SCRAMBLING GOLF

SCRAMBLING GOLF How to Get Out of Trouble and Into the Cup

by George Peper

PRENTICE-HALL, INC., Englewood Cliffs, N.J.

*SCRAMBLING GOLF: How to Get Out of
Trouble and Into the Cup* by George Peper

Prentice-Hall International Inc., London
Prentice-Hall of Australia, Pty. Ltd., Sydney
Prentice-Hall of Canada, Ltd., Toronto
Prentice-Hall of India Private Ltd., New Delhi
Prentice-Hall of Japan, Inc., Tokyo
Prentice-Hall of Southeast Asia Pte. Ltd., Singapore
Whitehall Books Limited, Wellington, New Zealand

10 9 8 7 6 5 4 3

Library of Congress Cataloging in Publication Data
Peper, George.
    Scrambling golf.
    Includes index.
    1. Golf.   I. Title.
GV965.P43 1977   796.352's   76-50070
ISBN 0-13-796672-5

ACKNOWLEDGMENTS

The author is indebted in several areas and to
many people. First, to the USGA and to Golf
Magazine for their splendid libraries. Secondly,
to the Spalding, Acushnet, and Foot-Joy
companies for use of their equipment in the
photographs. The excellent sequence photos
are the work of Ed Vebell, and the still shots
come from the lenses of two good friends,
Peter Bisconti and Chappie Morris. Ralph
Terry was a willing and flawless model, as was
David Fay, whose advice on the manuscript
was also helpful. And, my special thanks go to
Desmond Tolhurst for his generous counsel on
the final text and to Ben Crenshaw for his
kind contribution of the foreword.

"I have always said that I won golf tournaments because I tried harder than anyone else and was willing to take more punishment than the others. More immodestly, I will now say that I think a large factor in my winning was a greater resourcefulness in coping with unusual situations and in recovering from or retrieving mistakes."

—Bobby Jones, 1961

FOREWORD

I guess the perfect golfer is the one who never has to scramble at all. But I haven't yet seen the guy who can hit every fairway and every green. So what it boils down to is that we're *all* scramblers, to a greater or lesser degree, and the one who can save the most shots is the one who will win the tournament, be it the club championship or the U.S. Open.

I'm the first to admit that I've made my share of scrambling pars and birdies—even an eagle here and there. On some of those shots I may have looked pretty lucky, and maybe on a couple of them I was. But good scrambling is never a game of chance. It is the result of careful judgment, diligent practice, and experience with lots of different lies and situations. On the tour, scrambling is part of survival. You simply *must* know how to recover from a bad shot and attack when you've got an opening.

The same is true if you're a weekend golfer, only more so. Amateurs miss far more shots and get into far worse trouble than pros do. I'd guess that over 75 percent of the average golfer's strokes are played either from imperfect lies or from within a 50-yard radius of the cup. In amateur golf, scrambling is the name of the game, so it's a good idea to know what you're doing.

Besides, if you ever want to become a complete, truly accomplished golfer, you have to be able to do more than just hit a golf ball long and straight. You have to know how to make it talk. In order to progress from a mere golfer to a shot-maker you have to know how to hit it from right to left, left to right, high in the air, and low to the ground. And you had better be able to propel it from every type of lie, under all sorts of condtions, and from every corner of the golf course.

Scrambling Golf will show you how. If the shot isn't in this book, then it's probably not worth hitting. So do yourself a favor. Read these pages, practice these shots, and watch how your scores improve.

Ben Crenshaw
Austin, Texas

INTRODUCTION

It was Arnold Palmer who, several years ago, made one of the most clever and pointed remarks this side of St. Andrews. Arnie had just completed a pro-am round with Bob Hope. Palmer had shot a routine 68 while Hope had struggled to a score somewhere in the mid-80s. As they left the 18th green Hope turned to Palmer for encouragement.

"Well, Arnie, what do you think of my game?"

The reply was near poetic. "It's not bad, Bob, but I prefer golf."

Palmer's comment, though made in jest, says a great deal about the game of golf in America today. There are in fact *two* games—the one played by the touring professionals and the one played by the rest of us. Pro golf is a business and an art, requiring a unique combination of talent, temperament, and time. Amateur golf is a pastime, a mild form of exercise enjoyed by those of us who lack the strength, the skill, and the tenacity to tee it up on the tour. Our game is played with the same implements, under the same rules, and over the same terrain as pro golf, but there, quite abruptly, the resemblance ends.

The 99.9 percent of us whose game is amateur golf should therefore gear our efforts and interests on a decidedly different plane from those of Jack Nicklaus and company. This does not mean we should stop practicing. Quite the contrary, our practice should be more determined than ever, but it should be oriented productively and aimed at a realistic goal.

Most of us, after a year or so of golf experience, should abandon the search for the perfect swing. For once having learned the basics of the grip, stance, and hitting motions, we develop a swing-style that will probably never change in its essential character, no matter how much we fiddle with it. Besides, as amateurs we should be concerned with scoring, not swinging. We should leave the aesthetics to the pros and concentrate on the practical problem of getting the ball into the hole. After all, a perfect repeating swing isn't much help when your ball is sitting under a blackberry bush. And you'll find little solace from your 44-inch graphite driver when you have to make a 10-foot putt to win the nassau.

The saying "It's not how, it's how many" is old and trite, but like most old, trite sayings it makes a good point. For the most part, amateur golf has little to do with swing planes, pronated wrists, and 230-yard 2-irons. Amateur golf is a game of recovery shots and one-putt pars, a game of scrambling. It follows therefore that good scrambling is the amateur's fastest, most direct route to better golf.

Yet, sadly, few players care to think of themselves as scramblers. The problem undoubtedly begins with the fact that the word "scrambler" has always carried rather negative connotations. "Scrambler" conjures a vision of someone on all fours, groveling hurriedly to meet a deadline or to escape some threatening menace. One scrambles to catch a bus or to talk one's way out of a tax audit.

In golf this image has persisted for years. During the early '20s Henry Cotton "grew up to think of scrambling, i.e. getting up and down in two from every place, as poor class stuff." Coming from a highly accomplished professional, and an Englishman, this statement is understandable. For golf in Britain (and on the first American courses) placed a premium on skillful play from tee to green. Heavy rough lined the fairways and surrounded the putting surfaces, and the golfer who sprayed his shots was penalized severely. Recovery shots were strictly defensive propositions. One did one's best to get the ball back to the fairway, and then played to the green, accepting the inevitable loss of at least one shot along the way.

The greens themselves were not watered artificially as they are today, so golfers were unable to play the "bite" shots which make the ball check and spin back. The only reliable approach shot was the pitch and run, which rolled endlessly on the hard ground. The dry, undulating greens were generally much faster than those we know, and they forced players to be very cautious putters.

But times have changed, and the anti-scrambling game of Henry has gone the way of the rutt iron. In the 1920s Walter Hagen symbolized a new way to play golf. As perhaps the most aggressive and confident player in the history of the game, Hagen rarely let a difficult lie deter him from his appointed target. The Haig attacked a golf course as no one had before him, muscling the ball from the rough, bending it around the trees, and blasting it from the bunkers. In so doing he brought on a new era and a new kind of thinking in golf, where pars could be expected and made from anywhere on the course, not just the fairway.

As Hagen unveiled the scrambling game, innovations in golf course architecture and maintenance made that game easier for everyone to play. The American courses of today are less natural, less rugged than their ancestors. With a few notable exceptions, difficulty is based upon distance, not treachery. The rough is relatively light, at least compared to the heather and bracken of Britain's courses, and the greens are kept soft and true by constant watering and fertilization. As a result, golf scores have lowered, as better players have learned to tame the tall grass and play the delicate cuts and pitches that turn bogies into pars and pars into birdies.

Even on the pro tour, things have changed, as players like Palmer, Lee Trevino, and Ben Crenshaw have shown that low scores can come just as frequently through scrambling as through flawless, trouble-free play. The short game—chipping, sand play, and putting—has especially risen in importance on the tour. As recently as 20 years ago a pro was thought to be a wizard if he could limit himself to 33 putts for 18 holes. Today, the touring pro who averages 33 putts had better start looking for a club job.

So it's a bit ironic, isn't it? Scrambling is the game of today, yet few people want to be scramblers. We all get into trouble on the golf course, yet virtually none of us knows how to get out.

That's why this book was written. *Scrambling Golf* is a book of shots, some of which you may know, many of which you may never have considered, and all of which will help your game. In a way this is an "anti-instruction" book: There is no textbook method to learn, no miracle move to master. Instead, there is something better—a modern, efficient, and sensible approach to the game of amateur golf. I hope you'll find it useful.

G.P.
New York City

CONTENTS

SCRAMBLING GOLF

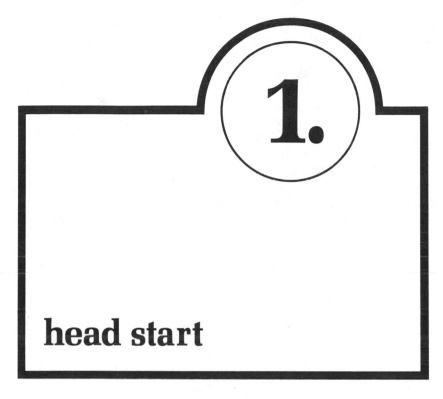

head start

KNOW THYSELF, IMPROVE THY GAME

Good scrambling begins with an unscrambled brain. Effective recovery shots and a consistently sharp short game depend upon mental poise, not physical skill. If you can keep your head together your game won't fall apart.

Socrates undoubtedly had scrambling golfers in the back of his mind when he said, "Know thyself." For in order to become a better trouble player, a better chipper and putter, or a better golfer in general, you must, at some point in your golfing career, sit down and make an honest, barefaced appraisal of your ability to play the game.

Handicap services help you to get some perspective, by printing a cold little number next to your name. Ultimately, however, your analysis must come from within, not from a computerized sheet. While your numbers and specifics will vary, your soliloquy should go something like this:

17

I am not Jack Nicklaus and I never will be. I am a 14-handicapper, which means that I'm neither a good player nor a bad one. Most of my scores will be between 83 and 90. Because of my recurrent slice I miss more fairways than I hit. My woods and irons are fairly accurate, if not as long as I'd like, but my chipping is terribly inconsistent. My fear of sand traps costs me two to three shots a round, and my unwillingness to work on my putting results in an average of 38 putts per 18 holes. Unless I'm willing to spend plenty of time and money on practice and lessons, I will never be much better than I am now.

Depressing as this self-analysis can be at first, it is the only way to develop a happy, well-adjusted, and productive approach to your game. If you have this clear and truthful view, you can make improvements in a number of ways.

First, that depression can lead to embarrassment which can lead to a dedication to pull yourself up. The feeling you'll get from this game assessment is not unlike the wince you experience when you step on the scale and realize you've gained twenty pounds. After the shock and chagrin wear off, you go on a diet. Such a "diet" for the serious golfer would be aimed at reducing his handicap through diligent practice of the weakest parts of his game.

If your analysis does not lead you to embarrassment, it will lead you to acceptance, and in that knowledge you'll improve. For if you can accept honestly the fact that you're a 14-handicapper, then you can also accept the inevitability of at least fourteen mistakes in each round you play. By being prepared for these disappointing shots, you won't react with the same unjustified anger, the same vain indignation most golfers show after making a boo-boo. Quite the contrary, if you're truly well adjusted to your game, you'll be able to view each successive mistake as an almost *positive* occurrence, in that it represents one less error you have left in your quota for the day.

This is a sense of serenity which is uncommon and invaluable on the golf course. In addition to changing you from a mere hacker to a happy hacker, it can have a salutory effect upon your score. For it stands to reason that when two high handicappers—one a golfer who knows his game and the other an unenlightened soul—hit into similar predicaments the player with an accurate self-view will acquit himself with the greater ease and effectiveness. Few attributes are more important to the scrambler than this ability to keep an untroubled head in trouble situations.

Begin by taking an honest look at your ability as a golfer.

No matter what your personal hole-by-hole strategy may be, you should think aggressively around the green.

Of course, an honest look at your golf game will reveal more than your weaknesses; it will bring to light your relative strengths as well. And no matter how meager your strong points may be, you will *know* what they are and you will *know* you have them, and through that positive knowledge you will find confidence.

Awareness of your inadequacies plus confidence in your strong points form the mental basis of the scrambling mentality, an approach that will enable you to get the most out of your game. If you know your strengths, weaknesses, and general tendencies with every club in the bag, then you don't have to work on your game in order to improve. You can make it work for you by matching it to the great diversity of golf shots you encounter.

You'll have the confidence to attack when the conditions favor your game. Just as important, however, you'll have the good sense to play conservatively when the situation calls for a "supershot" that just isn't in your bag of tricks. In a larger sense, you'll be able to map your strategy on a hole-by-hole basis and thereby establish a general plan of attack as we'll see in Chapter 9.

AGGRESSIVENESS

This blueprint will be different for every golfer, but for most golfers it will lead to a realization that is at the core of scrambling golf: The closer you are to the hole the more aggressive you should be.

The green is the place where shots are made up, where the mistakes of the fairway are erased by a good putt or a stiff chip. It takes only one good shot to make a par, and nine times out of ten that shot occurs near or on the green.

A 240-yard shot over water separates the pros from the duffers, but we are all equals over a 50-foot putt. The short game demands far less than full shots in terms of coordinated power. As such it can and should be developed by those of us who are not classic strikers of the ball. That is why over half of this book deals with the techniques of getting up and down.

OVERAGGRESSIVENESS AND HOW TO CHECK IT

Of course, even the highest self-confidence and aggressiveness in the world can be fruitless, or even dangerous, if it isn't channeled in some way. Case in point: Mr. Confidence himself, Arnold Palmer, who blew a seven-shot lead over the last nine holes of the 1966 U.S. Open at San Francisco's Olympic Country Club, and the next day lost in a playoff to Billy Casper. Confidence unguided is about as effective as a racehorse without a jockey.

Golfing confidence can be harnessed in only one way— through concentration. *The trick is to put a round's worth of positive thinking into each shot, one shot at a time.* Like the focusing lens of a camera, the golfer's concentration has an optimum "depth of field." When you're concentrating properly, your thoughts center on only one thing—the shot you're about to hit.

Once you establish your game plan and general plan of attack for each hole, never look ahead. Although it's hard, you should try to avoid thinking about your final score before you're finished playing. Don't project your total until you've written eighteen numbers on the scorecard. This was Arnie's fatal flaw in that '66 Open. As he came to Olympic's back nine, playing superbly and holding a seemingly insurmountable lead, Palmer turned his thoughts—almost justifiably—to the possibility of breaking Ben Hogan's 72-hole record for the tournament. In focusing on the record book, Arnie later admitted, he lost sight of the immediate concerns, holes nine through 18. Casper, of course, did not, and the rest is history. Arnie's game has never been the same since.

Your attention should never roam further forward than the

ideal placement for your next shot. Nor should you ever look back, because this is just as dangerous, if not worse. Over-pessimism due to your last shot can be as lethal as overoptimism about your next one.

If you have a bad first few holes, don't let your concentration flag. Take that positive approach mentioned earlier, and assume that the worst is behind you, that you've made your quota of mistakes and your best golf is just around the dogleg; then set about playing that kind of golf by taking one shot at a time and giving equal effort to every shot and every putt, whether it's for a birdie or a double bogey. When things get really bad, remember "the wee Scotsman," Bobby Cruickshank, who, at one point in the 1932 PGA, was 11 holes down with 12 to go. Yes, he won his match.

When you hit into trouble, don't lose your concentration, double it, because you'll need twice as much as you normally do. View trouble shots as a challenge to your scrambling sense and ability, and meet the challenge with everything you have.

HOW TO CONCENTRATE

Of course, scrambling concentration is far more than just a deter-mined state of mind. It is, in fact, a disciplined routine. In this respect, the mental side of scrambling is in direct contrast to the physical shot-making. In hitting trouble shots there is no re-peating swing, no list of checkpoints involved, because each unusual situation calls for a different type of swipe. Yet the mental technique follows a rigid, uniform regimen that should develop identically on every shot.

The mental how-to of scrambling moves through three distinct states: deciding on the proper shot, selecting the appro-priate club, and choosing the optimum swing.

You should begin focusing on your shot as soon as you know where your ball lies. First, ask yourself where you want to put your next shot. Remember, this spot, be it somewhere on the fairway or somewhere on the green, must be within reach of you and your game. Be sure to consider all the alternatives—left, right, center; short ball or big hit. After deciding on your goal you should be able to give yourself a good reason for wanting to hit to position A instead of B, C, D, or E.

Once you've approached your ball and you've decided where your next shot should go, ask yourself what the optimum route to your goal would be. Visualize your ball moving from your present lie to your desired lie. How high do you want or have to hit the ball? What about the bend of the shot—should it be straight, left-to-right, or right-to-left? Consider your lie, the distance you want to cover, the nature of the intervening terrain, the wind and weather conditions, and your standing in the match, if you're playing one. Remember, again, that you're choosing the most intelligent shot within your own capabilities, not Jack Nicklaus's. However, you should never let that awareness prevent you from considering all the possible shots.

Imagination is the scrambler's edge. Often, in order to hit out of trouble, you must first be inventive enough to *see* your way out. For instance, if your ball comes to rest twelve inches from a tree and the tree impedes your normal backswing, what should you do? Take an unplayable lie? Perhaps—but not before considering the through-the-legs shot, the reverse croquet shot, the slap shot, and the carom (all found in Chapter 5). One of these "trick shots" may actually be the percentage ploy, the wisest and most productive alternative. Imagination, tempered by your own self-awareness, can save you dozens of shots every year.

So consider *all* the alternatives, even those that may seem outlandish. Weigh the possible consequences, both good and bad, of the several available routes, and match the situation with the shot you feel is most promising.

Once you've decided where you want to go and how you want the shot to look, turn your thoughts toward choosing the best club for the job. Consider your trajectory and distance needs, your own power with each club, and your ability to make the various clubs work.

You'll find that if you've made the honest Socratic assessment of your game, you'll have relatively little trouble deciding on the optimum shot and club. In knowing your strengths and weaknesses you'll realize that certain shots will come easily and others won't come at all. If you know your good clubs and bad ones (and, let's face it, we all have both) you'll be able to make your club selections quickly, too.

Let's say, for instance, that you're a player of average power and your drive on a par-4 hole has come to rest in the fairway 180 yards from an unguarded green. Unfortunately, a huge tree in full bloom stands just 30 yards in front of you and in direct line with the green. Let's also assume that you have a natural fade. This should be enough to tell you to hit the ball left of the tree and let it come back in to the green. Now, what about the club? Well, you have 180 to go, normally a solid 2-iron shot, but you have very little confidence in your long irons. Besides, this one has to fade quite a bit so you'll lose some distance. Your answer is in the 4-wood, which you normally hit pretty well. Even if you have to shorten your grip a bit, the 4-wood is the club, because it's the one you know will get you home.

Having made a firm decision on the best shot to hit and the right club to use, center your concentration on the swing. First, visualize once more the path your ball must take. Then try to match that vision with a "swing-feeling." Take a practice swing—not just any swing, but a swing that feels as if it will do the job that has to be done. Occasionally this swing will require conscious adjustments of grip, stance, and swing plane. More often it will come naturally, especially if you've chosen your shot and club based on an honest evaluation of your game. When all systems are go, when you think you have a clear picture, the best club for the job, and a positive swing-feeling, then your confidence and concentration have blended well—go ahead and hit the shot.

While the three-part focus, as described here, may seem to be a structured and deliberate approach to golf, it is in practice a very smoothly moving mental continuum. Once you put it to work a few times you'll find that it comes very naturally and that, from beginning to end, it takes you very little time to "think out" your shot. If you know your game as you should, then you'll think confidently, clearly, and quickly.

The best example of this fast, efficient focusing is a fellow who is probably the number one thinker/shot-maker/scrambler on the pro tour, Lee Trevino. Concentration seems almost second nature to Supermex, who can turn it on and off with the flash of a smile. When he does turn it on, he doesn't fool around. With somber self-assurance he goes to work, swiftly stalking the shot and setting his stance. Once over the ball he wastes no time. He's confident that the shot he wants is in his mind, the club he wants is in his hand, and the swing he wants is in his body. Ninety-nine times out of a hundred, he's right. Trevino's well-paced performance is a model for us all.

As you can see from the foregoing discussion of mental philosophy and technique, scrambling golf is not what it connotes. Although the dictionary defines "scrambling" as "an urgent, confused, unceremonious struggle for something," this game within the game of golf is entirely different. Scrambling golf is a smart, careful, and deliberate game that demands a full measure of thought and discipline from any golfer who chooses to play it well.

Scrambling is not gambling, because the true scrambler always makes the right bet. He views all the possibilities and then selects the option that offers him the greatest chance of success. Sometimes it may seem to be the long shot, at others, a sure thing, but it is always the best shot for him.

Most books of golf instruction begin with several chapters on the elements of the golf swing, and conclude with a word or two about the mental side of golf. Their purpose is to first equip you with the important fundamentals and then to fine-tune your ability by teaching you how to think effectively.

The organization of this book is exactly the opposite, and yet the philosophy is the same. The bases of scrambling golf are mental, and they have been presented first. Each of the trouble shots and short shots to follow will pose a different problem, calling for a unique physical response. Mentally, however, every shot will be played the same way. This is because effective scrambling begins in the mind; aptitude grows from attitude.

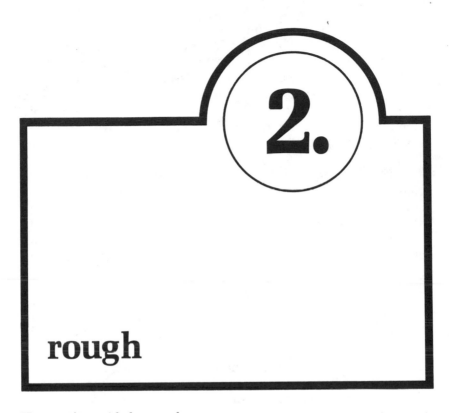

rough

You can't avoid the rough.

You can fly the trees, hop the creeks, roll through the traps, and skitter across the ponds, but you can't skirt that heavy grass that lines the fairways. All golf courses have rough, whether its height is two inches or two feet, and every golfer finds it, whether his handicap is 1 or 31. Even among the touring pros it is rare for a player to complete 18 holes without straying into the rhubarb. So when your ball settles half-hidden into heavy rough, take heart—you have just experienced the most common aberration from golf's straight and narrow path.

Since we hit into the rough with such ease and regularity, you'd think we'd be able to extricate ourselves without too much pain, that we'd at least be able to limit ourselves to one shot out for every shot in. Such, of course, is not the case. In fact, amateur golfers waste more strokes flailing through high grass than anywhere else on the course.

Part of the problem, as always, is psychological. Faced with a deep, shaggy lie, most of us react in one of two ways—over-pessimistically or overoptimistically. The first type of golfer chokes with fear as he approaches his ball. By the time he is ready to swing this defeatist is consumed by the certainty that he won't get the ball out—and often, as a result, his fears prove to be well founded. The other guy is the one who thinks he's King Kong. He swaggers into the thickage with his 2-iron, eyes the pin some 200 yards away, and then beats at the ball with his "power swing," a roundhouse swipe that usually produces a shot of three to six feet.

Of course, neither paranoia nor overconfidence is appropriate when playing out of the rough. Curiously, however, the proper frame of mind *is* a blend of fear and machismo, though each is tempered a bit. The correct attitude is best expressed in the old phrase used by high school basketball coaches at pregame interviews: cautious optimism. When in the rough you should combine a respect for the difficulty of your lie with a firm belief in your ability to handle it.

This brings us to the other half of the problem, the physical business of "getting out." Success from the rough depends largely upon two things. You must first apply the concentration technique mentioned in Chapter 1. Make an accurate assessment of the situation so that you can match it with the appropriate shot. Secondly, you have to be able to hit that shot with both firmness and finesse. Stated simply, you choose the right shot and then you hit the right shot right.

Deciding on the best shot to hit from the rough is a bit more complicated than choosing a shot from the fairway. When your ball is in the fairway you have comparatively few things to worry about. Nine times out of ten the lie is excellent, so you don't have to concern yourself unduly with making clean contact. Most of us will consider only our distance from the green and whether or not there is any trouble to cross along the way. Better players will note wind direction and pin placement as well. That's usually enough.

In the rough there is a lot more to ponder. You should take into account everything you'd normally consider for a fairway shot—distance, topography, wind, pin placement. But in addition you must inspect the delicate and important position of your ball. What sort of rough is it in—sparse, moderate, or thick? What about the height of the grass—is it short, medium, or tall? Is the ball buried, sitting way up, or suspended somewhere in between? And the grass just in front of the ball—is it heavy? And if so, does it grow toward your destination or back toward your ball? How many yards of rough must you cross before you get back to the fairway? All of these questions, and occasionally a couple more, must be answered before you can make a competent and confident assessment of your plight.

Once you've made that appraisal and decided on the kind of shot you'll have to hit, your most important move will be selecting the proper club. This becomes simpler when you consider that, for most of us, only seven clubs—half those in the golf bag—may be used safely from the rough. The clubs are the 5-, 6-, 7-, 8-, and 9-irons, the wedge, and the 4-wood. This may seem like conservative advice, especially coming from a book on scrambling, but remember, scrambling isn't the same as gambling. Besides, there's nothing conservative about hitting a 5-iron or 4-wood from the rough.

There are 5-iron lies, 7-iron lies, 4-wood lies, but, for the most of us, there is rarely such a thing as a 2-iron or 3-wood lie in the rough. The weekend golfer, unless he is possessed of unusually strong limbs or, more important, a solid, vertical, pile-driving swing, cannot expect to get the ball up and sailing from rough with a low-lofted club. Sure there are "exceptions." Every golfer is lucky enough to get a beautiful lie in the rough now and then—with the ball sitting up smartly on a short, taut, well-clipped area of grass. In these cases it's fine to go ahead with a steep-faced club. But this is not a typical rough lie any more than a ball in a divot is a typical fairway lie. These are rubs of the green, and you should not let your experiences with them lead you to believe you can do the impossible with a 2-iron from the thick stuff. By and large, you can find 90 percent of your rough clubs in the forward half of your golf bag.

Not only is it *foolish* to try to hit a long iron from the rough; it is rarely necessary. A ball struck properly from light or moderate rough will rise faster, fly higher, and roll farther than a fairway shot hit with the same club. As a result, your 5-iron shot from the rough will cover nearly the same distance as your 3-iron shot from the fairway. Witness the 190-yard miracle performed by tour rookie Jerry Pate on the last hole of the 1976 U.S. Open. Pate's 5-iron out of the rough sailed high and long over a large pond fronting the Atlanta Athletic Club's home hole, and stopped less than three feet from the stick, guaranteeing him victory.

From time to time a pro or top amateur will hit into light rough intentionally, knowing that the extra height or distance he'll get can make the difference between hitting and missing the green. So, while a lie in tall grass is seldom a happy occurrence, it can be a blessing in disguise, if you know how to deal with it.

Let's take a look at a few good, bad, and worse situations in the rough, and match them to the shots they require.

Assume that you're in the rough and that you have a long way to go to the green, but your path is wide open and free of hazards and your lie is rated "PG"—pretty good. The ball is in light to moderate rough (relatively thin grass that is not more than four inches high) and is sitting fairly well, neither perched nor buried.

This is commonly called a "flyer" lie because of its tendency to produce a shot that takes off more quickly and soars higher and farther than a fairway shot hit with the same stick. The extra height and distance occur because blades of grass come between your club and ball at impact, inhibiting your normal ability to put backspin on the ball. The inevitable result is a spinless shot that flies like a knuckleball and bounces and rolls like a superball.

Under these conditions you should probably go ahead and take a pop at the ball with your 4-wood. It's not a hard shot, despite what many amateur golfers think.

The 4-Wood Shot

Although the 4-wood's physical design is not exactly scythelike, it is often more effective than its iron-faced cousins in getting the ball up and out of reasonable rough. With its heavy head and

From a moderate or good lie in the rough, go ahead and try a 4-wood or 5-wood. The wood's smooth, heavy head moves through thick grass far more easily than do the long irons.

smooth, rounded sole, the 4-wood will slide through grass with much less resistance than the thin, light blade of a 2- or 3-iron, which will invariably be turned or deflected by the clinging greenery. Besides, on the fairway most of us feel more comfortable with a 4-wood than with a low iron. Why change gears in the rough?

At this point it should be noted that a 5-wood is just as good as, and in some ways even better than, a 4-wood for rough shots. The 5-wood has all the positive features of the 4-, plus the advantage of 3 degrees more loft. So if you have trouble with your low irons and you get along well with the 4-wood, consider trading in your 2- or 3-iron for a 5-wood. It's a useful club from the fairway as well as the rough. If you need more convincing, consider Raymond Floyd's success with the 5-wood during the 1976 Masters tournament which he won by nine shots. Using his 5-wood on Augusta's par-5s Floyd made three pars, an eagle and 12 birdies for a record 14 under par on the long holes.

The 4-wood (or 5-wood) from rough should be hit a bit differently than from the fairway. Your objective is to minimize the effect of rough, to make a swing which involves as little contact as possible between your club and the grass. This type of shot calls for an upright, vertical swing, beginning with a fast-rising takeaway and culminating in a steep, descending blow to the back-bottom quadrant of the ball (this descending blow will ensure the sharply *ascending* shot you need). Since the normal fairway 4-wood is hit with a long, low takeaway and a resulting sweep through the ball, an adjustment should be made when you're standing in longer grass.

This does not mean you have to make a conscious effort to overhaul your swing every time you want to hit a 4-wood from the rough. A small change in your stance will set you up automatically for the correct pass at the ball. All you have to do is stand an inch or two closer to the ball. This move alone will promote the vertical swing that results in the descending hit at impact. If you want even more insurance, you can "move up" on the ball a bit by playing it an inch farther back in your stance than normal.

One important thought, however, with regard to your address position: Don't ground your club, no matter what kind of lie you have. There are at least three reasons for this. First, by keeping your club away from the ball, you'll eliminate the risk of moving or causing a twig or piece of grass to move it and thus

cost you a penalty stroke. Secondly, by starting your backswing from an off-the-ground position, you will reduce the chance of catching your club on the backswing. Thirdly, holding your club off the ground will force you to lift it sooner on your takeaway and thus make a more vertical swing, which is the whole object of the shot.

If you want another reason not to ground your club, consider the fact that a couple of players named Nicklaus and Trevino never ground their clubs at address—not in the rough, not on the fairway. Watch closely next time—Jack doesn't even ground his putter!

Back to that 4-wood shot. Using your vertical stance, make a smooth, unaffected backswing and a good firm move back into the ball. Don't swing hard, just be firm. Since the grass, no matter how thin and shallow, is bound to give some resistance, it's important that you hit down forcefully. Lead the club through with your hands and be sure to make a full follow-through—don't let the club die in the weeds.

You'll find that if you can hit your 4-wood effectively and consistently, over half of your rough game will be in good shape. The 4-wood from rough can give capability over a tremendous range. With a flyer lie you can hit it as long as any 2-wood from the fairway. On the other hand, by gripping down on it a bit you can use it for much shorter shots. With favorable lies and wide-open holes the golfer with average power can use the 4-wood for shots of anywhere from 175 yards up—which makes the old cleek a pretty versatile tool.

Iron Shots

One way of defining the situations that call for an iron shot is to describe the occasions that prohibit using the 4-wood. The most obvious limiting factor is distance. Never use a 4-wood if your landing area is tight or narrow. The risk of hitting an errant flyer is not worth the extra distance. Play safe with the 5-iron, no

The 4-Wood from Rough: Stand about an inch closer to the ball than you would for a fairway shot, and play the ball about an inch farther back in your stance than normal. This will set you up for the vertical takeaway and the firm descending blow to the ball. At impact your hands should be forward of the ball, as they were at address. Follow through fully to ensure maximum distance.

From flyer lies such as this one, take one club less than you would for a fairway shot of the same distance, e.g., take a 6-iron instead of a 5.

matter how good your lie may be. Also, don't pull out a 4-wood if your ball is in long or thick grass.

Once again, let's begin by assuming you have a pretty good lie—neither great nor terrible. The special problems posed by thick and fluffy lies will be covered later.

In selecting your iron for a shot from rough, take a good look at the distance you have to cover, ask yourself what club you'd hit if you were on the fairway, and then take one club *less*. Remember, if you make solid contact with a ball in a flyer lie, the resultant shot will give you more distance than the same shot hit from clipped grass. Also, with regard to your immediate problem, getting up and out of the weeds, the more lofted club is better, both functionally and psycholgically. If you think you can get out with a 5-iron then you will *know* you can get out with a 6-iron.

Don't forget to consider the nature of the terrain your recovery shot will be crossing. When you face a middle-distance shot to a green guarded by traps or water and backed by the same or by out-of-bounds, you probably shouldn't try to throw a full shot from the rough directly to the putting surface. A flyer shot, especially a longish one, does not always stop on the same green it lands on. So in some cases the wisest move is to play your recovery shot short of the hazard and then chip onto the green. In golf as in life, discretion is the better part of valor.

One more word of caution: Don't expect to be able to "maneuver the ball" from rough. You can hook, draw, slice and fade from the fairway because your club is able to make clean, flush contact with the ball and impart the necessary spin. But in the rough, that intervening grass strips your shot of all spin. So if you want to go right or left from rough, you had better aim yourself accordingly. If you don't have that option, or if, for instance, a tree is in your way, then you'd better play safe, because there's no way you'll ever hit a big bender from a flyer lie.

The basic principle for hitting iron shots from rough is the same as it is for the 4-wood. You want the club to have a minimum of contact with the grass. This, again, means using an upright swing, where the club rises quickly and descends sharply to the ball.

As with the 4-wood, the major shift involves your ball position, which should be slightly farther back than normal. Note: It may seem strange that, in order to achieve a fast-rising shot, you must play the ball back in your stance where the club catches it on the downswing. Granted, the effective loft of the clubface will be reduced slightly when you make this adjustment, but don't let that worry you. Remember, you're using a more lofted club than you would from the fairway, and that alone will cancel the de-lofting effect. Secondly, if you make that downward hit on a ball in a flyer lie, be assured that your ball will rise nearly as fast as a wedge shot hit off your left toe!

Use your normal alignment and grip, but hold onto the club a bit more tightly than you would for a fairway shot. The firm grip is necessary because the grass has a nasty tendency to wrap around the hosel of your club and close the face. In especially thick, clingy rough it's a good idea to allow for that club-closing effect by addressing the ball with a slightly open clubface. That way, the grass will close the club into a square position at impact.

Your swing should follow the same tempo as the 4-wood swing—a slow, deliberate backswing followed by a firm, descending blow to the ball. In making the swing, remember a couple of things: First, keep most of your weight on your left side at address, and never shift that weight totally on the backswing. This will help you to lean down and into the shot. Concentrate on pulling your left hand down and through the ball, and be sure to hang on tight throughout impact and follow-through. A couple of quick practice swings here will be helpful. You'll get a good idea of what you're up against when you swing the club back and through the grass.

When you get a lie like this one, remember that your first objective is to get the ball out. Then you can worry about hitting up to the stick. Don't try to do both in one shot unless you're very close to the green.

Heavy Rough

When you find yourself in serious rough, you had better know how to handle it or it will surely handle you. Bad trouble in the rough can come in at least three ways. You can have a buried lie in moderate rough, a so-so lie in deep rough, or a bad lie in deep rough. Whichever fate befalls you, your game plan should be the same.

Be mindful that your first objective is to get the ball out. Unlike most rough lies, a buried ball is not a flyer it's a floater, which means that at impact it will take off more like a blimp than a rocket. Unless you're shooting from very close range, you should forget about hitting for the green, and just try to get the ball back to the fairway.

You'll have to use one of your most lofted clubs—the 8-iron, 9-iron, or wedge—with the wedge the wisest choice, especially if you're just playing it safe. However, if the situation offers a glimmer of hope, you might try one of the other two. In any case, focus your attention more on your lie than on your destination, and be damn sure that the club you choose will get

The Mid-Iron from Rough: Play the ball well back in your stance so that your hands are ahead and most of your weight is on your left side. On the backswing the weight shift is minimal, and on the way down your left hand should pull the club down and through the grass. In heavyish lies, open the clubface a couple degrees at address to compensate for the club-closing effect of the grass.

you up and out. If you think you can do it with the 8-iron, then by all means go ahead—and hit the *9-iron*.

The technique for dealing with these U.S. Open lies is simply an exaggeration of the principles used for light and moderate rough. You want a supervertical swing, in order to avoid mowing through too much grass, and to raise the ball quickly out of the high grass. Assuming you take the wedge, play the ball back off your right heel, open your stance a bit, and open your clubface a few degrees, to compensate for the closing effect the grass will have.

Grip the club firmly and take that rough-shooting swing, being sure to pull down hard on the ball. Don't be afraid to beat at it in these tough lies. The deeper your lie, the steeper and more forceful your swing should be. Again, a couple of practice swings are in order. And one final thought in making these unorthodox shots: Don't lose sight of golf's golden rule—keep your head down, or you'll never get the ball up.

Unusual Lies

The buried ball's direct opposite, the ball sitting up high in rough, is perhaps the most deceptive lie in golf. Invariably, a golfer will view this lie as a lucky break—a perfectly teed ball in the rough. Sometimes he'll be right, but more often he will be completely mistaken. He'll treat the lie in an overconfident, cavalier manner and will usually pay the penalty for this lack of knowledge and respect. In truth, the perched ball can be as treacherous and demanding as any lie you'll encounter, and it deserves a good deal of care and caution.

You should first inspect the lie carefully to determine the height to which it is perched. In doing this, tread softly and be careful not to dislodge the ball, unless you want an extra stroke on your card.

If the ball is sitting up high on top of the rough, you should guard against hitting under it, causing a pop fly, or even a whiff. Consequently, you will not want to make that steep blow you use for other rough shots. Instead your club must enter the impact area on a very shallow, almost level, angle.

The Wedge from Heavy Rough: Position the ball back off your right heel, and open both your clubface and your stance slightly. Your backswing should be full but not overly long. You can beat down hard on this shot, but keep a steady head through impact if you want to unearth the ball.

Begin by addressing the ball at its own height, whether it's an inch or a foot off the ground. This means choking up on your club (and, in this case, your club may be any of the fourteen, except the putter). Again, be careful in addressing and waggling that you don't topple the ball from its perch.

Your one necessary swing adjustment is this—take the club back long and low. (Just as a fast-rising takeaway promotes a steep downswing, a low, level takeaway will result in the smooth horizontal sweep you want.) Do your best to drag the club back, even if the grass gets in your way, although it shouldn't be too much of a factor, since your club should be fairly high in the air at address.

If you want just one more trick to ensure solid impact with a perched ball, here it is: Keep your left shoulder higher than your right. By addressing the ball with a high left shoulder and keeping it higher than usual throughout your swing, you'll be certain to take full advantage of the lie.

Yet another variable to consider when hitting out of rough is the direction of growth of the grass around and in front of your ball. If this grass is growing in the same direction you want

When the grass grows with your shot, expect lots of flight, bounce, and roll, and prepare yourself by taking two clubs less than you would from the fairway. Hit a 7-iron instead of a 5.

When hitting against the direction of growth of the grass, open your stance and clubface, and do your best to cut the ball up and out.

to go, you should be ready for a superflyer with lots of carry and bounce. Accordingly, you should consider taking two less clubs instead of just one.

Conversely, if the grass is growing against you, things are going to be a bit tougher, no matter what kind of rough you're in. Be prepared, in these situations, to bear down with the vertical swing. If you're in heavy stuff, open your wedge wide and do your best to get your club down hard and under the ball.

Finally, the species of grass you're dealing with can make a difference in the way your shot will behave. Bermuda grass, found mostly on Southern courses, is a far stronger, tougher, and coarser grass than bent or blue grass. Your club will meet more resistance in Bermuda, and you should adjust accordingly. Respect it, by taking a more lofted club from moderate and deep lies, and swinging with a little extra firmness whenever grass clings to your ball.

Of course, the rough, troublesome as it may be, is a comparatively mild penalty, a friendly warning that more sadistic perils await the golfer who sprays his shots. Chapter 3 tells you more about the many variations of double-trouble and how to deal with them.

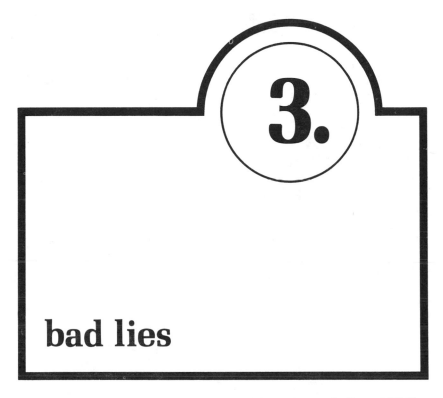

bad lies

Golf balls turn up in the strangest places. Just ask Cary Middle-coff, who one day discovered that his teeshot had come to rest on top of a coiled-up snake. Or Tony Jacklin, whose drive took one bounce and landed in the back pocket of a guy playing in front of him. Or Tom Weiskopf, who, during a recent U.S. Open, found his ball next to a dozen hot dog rolls on the shelf of a concession stand.

And these are the pros—who are known for their ability to keep the ball in play. Amateur golfers, for whom "the unusual is usual," have reported some even stranger lies. Golf balls have been found in bottles, in cans, and in cups of tea. In beehives, bird's nests, rabbit hutches, and (several) under setting hens. On the back of a sheep and in the ear of a horse. They've rolled up drain pipes and dropped down chimneys. They've sailed through the windows of moving cars, trucks, trains, buses, and even a helicopter. Yes, since the days of the gutta-percha the golf ball has found its way into about every imaginable place. One remarkable teeshot has even come back to rest on the very same wooden peg from which it was propelled.

41

Of course, some of these strange lies are less strange than others, and it behooves all golfers to know how to handle the more recurrent pests. That's what this chapter is about.

The instruction which follows won't tell you how to feather a 6-iron from the back of a crocodile or hit a flip wedge from the roof of the caddy hut. It will, however, give you the capability to deal confidently with several of golf's cruel and unusual punishments. Divots, tufts and clover, hardpan, fairway traps, pine needles and leaves, water, sandy rough, and the various hilly lies will all be cut down to size and negotiated, one by one. In essence, this chapter will show you how to play shots from *all over the golf course*, since that, after all, is where most of us find ourselves.

Strange as it may seem, some of the game's worst lies lurk right in the middle of the fairway. If you play winter rules, which allow you to improve your fairway lies, you have no worries here, but if you play golf as it was meant to be played, you should know how to deal with divots, clover, and thick fairway lies.

Divots

To most of us, there's nothing more discouraging than to pound a drive 250 yards down the center of the fairway and then discover that the ball has come to rest in the middle of a six-inch divot. This is the time, more than any other, to keep your head. Sure, you want to kick your golf bag, or the guy who failed to replace the divot, or at least kick the ball out of the hole it's in, but don't do any of these things. When your ball settles in a divot—or in any small depression—chalk it up to bad luck and forget it. Then put a couple of simple concepts to work, and you'll still make good use of that teeshot.

The only thing to remember when hitting out of a divot is to *hit down* on the ball, not scoop it out. In this respect, the divot swing is similar to the rough swing and to the swings for many trouble shots to follow—you hit *down* to get the ball up and out.

In order to assure this down-and-out action, take your address so that the ball is an inch or so back of its normal position in your square stance. In so doing you should catch the ball at the end of your downswing while the club is still descending and thus sting it out of the divot.

Sure it's disappointing to find that your long, straight drive has found its way into a divot, but don't lose your cool. There's no reason why you still can't take advantage of a good shot.

It's a good idea to close the face of your club just a degree or two, because the jolt of impact with the dirt will open the face. By closing the face a little at address you'll assure yourself of square contact with the ball. Before swinging make a couple of practice takeaways to be sure you can bring the club smoothly past the divot's edge. If you find that the club bumps the divot, don't be afraid to compensate by breaking your wrists quickly and raising the club early in your backswing. This adjustment will help achieve the descending blow you want.

Keep your swing relatively short, about three-quarters the normal length, and focus your eyes on the front half of the ball. This will help ensure that the club comes down directly on the *back* half of the ball, not behind it or on one of the edges of the divot. The key hitting-down mechanism is the hands, which must lead the club down crisply through the ball. Keep a good tight grip on the club as you pull into the divot, and hold your wrists stiff throughout impact and follow-through. If your ball is resting against the outside edge of the divot, adjust by closing the face of your club a couple of degrees at address. If it's against the inside edge, do the opposite—open your clubface a bit. These compensations will allow you to bang the ball out of the divot without it caroming off the edge on the way.

One last note: Never use a wood from a divot, no matter how far you are from the fairway and how much confidence you have in your woods. The long shafts and blunt soles of woods make them impractical divot diggers. Hitting out of a small patch of dirt with a wood is a low-percentage shot, and no scrambler in his right mind would try it.

It's never lucky to have a lie in clover, not even the four-leafed variety. Fortunately, there are several ways to deal with this lie. One of them (right) is to hit the punch shot.

Clover and Fluffy Lies

Divots aren't the only pests that can sabotage a good drive. Just as common as these bare scrubs are their exact opposites—the fluffy, overly thick lies.

Many of us fail to recognize the fact that a ball sitting in clover or on a tuft of grass is not a good lie. Like a perched ball in rough, the situation looks good, with the ball sitting up fat and sassy. However, a lie in tufts or clover is rarely lucky, even if the clover is four-leafed. The long grass and slick tendrils of clover tend to slip between the clubface and the ball. As with lies in the rough, the intervening greenery inhibits your ability to impart backspin to the ball, and causes a high, wobbly shot with abnormally long flight and bounce.

After you've hit a few of these flyers you'll begin to suspect bushy lies for the culprits they are, and you'll realize that a couple of quick adjustments are advisable.

Actually, there are several ways of coping with tufted/clover lies. First is the "If you can't beat 'em, join 'em" philosophy: Just take one club less than you normally would, give it your usual swing, and let the high flyer carry you the needed distance.

Your second choice is at the opposite extreme—to minimize the flyer effect by hitting a punch shot. Again, take a club less, and hit a compact, stiff-wristed shot. Keep your hands out in front of the ball at impact, and throw them right at the flag on your follow-through. This low, running approach is, of course, impractical if traps, water, or any trouble fronts the green.

The third and most sophisticated method of extrication from thick fairway is to try to produce a normal shot from these abnormal lies. To do this you must hit the ball the same way you would a perched ball in the rough—with a shallow sweep into the ball. Take your normal alignment and grip, but choke down on the club a bit and address the top of the ball. Also, stand so that your left shoulder is higher than your right. Your only swing thought should be to concentrate on making a long, low take-away, delaying your wrist cock as long as possible. This should promote a good horizontal movement into the ball on your downswing, a movement which should compensate for the treachery of the lie and give you as good a shot as one hit from a perfect lie.

If you should be unfortunate enough to land an inch or so in back or in front of a large, unruly tuft of grass, do one thing and one thing only—play it safe. If you're just in back of a tuft, chip over it or to the side. Don't try to go through it. That harmless-looking grass, if it catches your ball just after impact, will divert it as quickly and effectively as a brick wall. If you find yourself just past a very stubby tuft, it's normally unwise to try to swing through it to the ball. You're better advised to move your swing around it, opening or closing the club to compensate, and chip to a better lie. Above all, keep your cool—no matter how bad a break you get. And even when playing it safe, play carefully. Think out your shot, and concentrate on putting the most into it and getting the most out of it.

Hardpan

If your teeshot should stray from the fairway onto a worn path or dirt road paralleling the fairway, you'll probably be hitting your second shot from hardpan. Most golfers would rather be in the rough.

However, before you curse at a lie in hardpan, remember that it is not without its virtues. When an arching, well-directed drive makes its first bounce on one of those firm, dry scabs of dirt, the ball often takes a huge leap forward. Thanks to hardpan, many of us average players have hit 300-yard drives, and a 300-yard drive is usually worth the scuff on the ball. Nonetheless hardpan brings to mind the old postcard phrase "It's a nice place to visit, but you wouldn't want to live there." It's nice to bounce on it as long as you bounce off it.

Better strikers of the ball can do magic with a hardpan lie. In reality, hard, bare ground is not a bad place to be if you hit the ball purely and consistently, because in such a grassless lie you can put plenty of lateral spin on the ball, and play the intentional fades and draws described in the next chapter. For most of us, however, the hardpan shot is a defensive one that demands more than a little scrambling.

The first thing you should check is the back of the scorecard. A local rule may entitle you to relief in the form of a free drop. Be on the lookout for any indication of ground under repair, too. There's no reason to tax your game (and your equipment) unnecessarily.

The shot from hardpan is similar to the divot shot in that your club must strike the ball first and then the ground. If you hit the ground first, the club will bounce up and you'll surely top the ball.

To hit this pinching punch shot, take a square stance with the ball back farther than normal and your hands well forward of the ball. If you're also standing on hardpan, be sure your footing is good. Take a couple of practice cuts just to be certain. If necessary, widen your stance for a steadier swing. If your footing isn't absolutely rock steady, you'll never catch the ball with the precision this shot demands.

Keep your eye on the front half of the ball—this way you'll hit the back of it instead of hitting it fat, a disaster from hardpan. Your backswing should be as steady as your stance, a smooth, stiff-wristed three-quarter swing. Be deliberate on the downswing and let your hands and wrists lead through and out at the flag.

Since this shot is normally a low-flying runner, take one club less than you need for the distance. It will give you added loft and stop and no less distance. Also, lay off the wood clubs. This lie is just too thin for them.

When you pull off the hardpan shot your playing partners

From Hardpan: Take one club less than normal, address the ball well back in your square stance, and pull down into impact with your left hand. Keep your wrists firm, and don't let your right hand roll over your left until well after you've hit the ball.

Fairway trap lies are rarely as awesome as most golfers imagine them to be.

will surely raise their eyebrows. And after you've done it right once you'll never worry about it again—well, at least not until you get another bare lie.

Fairway Traps

If you're like most golfers, you cringe or swear or do both when you find that your drive has found its way into a fairway trap. A hundred and seventy yards to go and there you are in the middle of a craterful of sand!

Granted, fairway traps aren't normally as friendly as fairways, but they're at least manageable, and in most cases they pose little problem at all. As with many trouble spots, the major obstacle is in your mind, not in your lie.

It's fine to respect fairway traps, but there's no reason to fear them. Remember, the majority of fairway traps are reasonably large and flat, which means that unless you're up against the lip you'll probably be able to take a full, balanced, unhampered swing at the ball. Secondly, it's rare for a drive to burrow into the sand of a fairway trap. Most teeshots either land in the trap and take a small bounce or two or land outside the trap and roll in gently. In either case, the resulting lie is likely to be a good one, assuming the trap is raked and in proper condition. Fairway

From a Fairway Trap: Take a wide, firm, square stance, grip down an inch on the club, and concentrate on hitting solidly into the back of the ball. Keep your lower body relatively "quiet," and make a three-quarter swing, using one club more than you'd use from the fairway.

traps rarely serve up those fried eggs and buried balls so common to bunkers around the green, where the ball usually enters the sand from a steeper angle.

What you'll probably find is a ball sitting up nicely, with no great lip to hurdle, and an open shot to the green—nothing to worry about, really, if you select the right club and give it a strategic swing.

When choosing your club, you should probably forget the wood clubs, no matter how far you have to go, unless all of the following are true: (1) You have an excellent lie; (2) There is virtually no lip on the trap and no obstruction between you and the green; and (3) Your handicap is 10 or less. If you 20-handicappers want to hit the ball 200 yards, try a 2-iron. If you want 20 feet, pick a wood. Seriously, choose an iron and take one club more than you would for a fairway shot of equal distance.

The first thing to do is dig in deep. Step into the trap with confidence. Too many players tiptoe in as if they were entering a minefield. Make your stance a little wider than for a fairway shot, and don't be afraid to grind your feet down into the sand— this will ensure good footing. Next, because you lower your stance when you dig in, choke up an inch on your club. (This shortened shaft is one of the reasons you need more club.)

The swing for a fairway trap does not differ a great deal from the routine fairway-shot swing. Just bear a couple of concepts in mind. First, be aware that you cannot afford to hit behind the ball. As in the divot and hardpan shots, you have to hit the ball first. Unlike those shots, however, you don't want to hit down on the ball. Your effort should be to *sweep* the ball off the sand, which means that you want to hit solidly into the back of the ball and pick it cleanly off the sand. To do that, don't change anything in your swing. Just concentrate on making your own swing work as accurately as possible. Look at the forward half of the ball, and take the club back slowly and not too far. Don't try to make a big pivot or use a lot of leg action, because it won't be possible when you're ankle-deep in sand. Just take a three-quarter swing and do your best to bring the sweet spot of your club smoothly into the ball.

You'll often hear or read the advice that you should hit a controlled fade from fairway traps. The thinking is that the fade stance and swing promote the clean picking action and the immediate trajectory desirable for long sand shots. For most players, however, this is very bad counsel. Weekend golfers have enough trouble dealing with traps—they shouldn't have to worry about doctoring the shot. In addition, if you play an intentional fade, you have to take one club more than usual. This means that in a fairway trap you'll need *two* clubs more, and for most of us that's a significant switch. Nine out of ten golfers hit a 5-iron better than they hit a 3-iron.

So forget the fade. Take your own stance (though a bit wider), your own swing (though a bit easier), and hit the ball cleanly and squarely. You'll do just fine.

It's easy to assume blithely that all your fairway trap lies will be good—and many of them will be—but you'll also draw your share of bad lies. So you might as well know how to deal with the double jeopardy of having a sloppy lie in a fairway trap.

Embedded in a Fairway Trap
Let's assume your ball is partially embedded in a trap and you're still a good 6-iron's distance from the green. The nature of your lie should tell you that even your career 6-iron won't get you home. Solution? Take a 4-iron and hit a "distance explosion" shot. If the lip of the trap isn't in your way, this shot can be very effective.

The distance explosion does call for a couple of the fader's adjustments. As you dig in, open your stance, by pulling your left foot back about two inches from the target line. The swing should be slow and controlled, with your goal the same as it is in a normal fairway trap shot—to make as clean contact as possible with the ball. Don't take any more sand than you're forced to take by the lie. Finally, keep your wrists stiff throughout your follow-through. If all goes well, this will produce a sandy, fading 4-iron that will give you about the same distance as a clean 6-iron from the fairway.

Keep in mind that club selection is tricky with these partially sand-covered shots. You can take more club only up to a certain point. When you get a lie that's more than half buried, don't press your luck with the distance explosion. Go to one of the short irons and play safe. In cases where your lie and your distance to go tell you that you can't reach the green in one, it is best to loft a cagy shot to the fairway and hit an uncomplicated iron shot to the green rather than try to go for a big hit from the trap.

Be careful when taking a stance on a ball lying in leaves or pine needles. You could easily set off a chain reaction that would dislodge the ball and cost you a penalty stroke.

From a sandy lie: Make everything firm—your stance, your grip, and your downward stroke to the ball.

Debris

If you're the type of golfer who tends to take the scenic route from tee to green, you should know how to deal with lies in leaves, pine needles, pebbles, and roots.

When you have a lie in leaves or pine needles, forget everything you've ever read (here and elsewhere) about approaching a lie with brisk confidence. Not that these lies are so treacherous you should cower at the sight of them. It's just that if you're playing according to the Rules you should be very careful when stepping near your ball. Droppings, leaves, pine needles, twigs, and other natural debris have a tendency, when stepped on, to set off a chain reaction which can reach your ball and cause it to move. This would mean a penalty of one stroke.

If you're careful, you may be able to improve your lie by removing any "loose impediments," as the rulebook calls them. These are "natural objects not fixed or growing and not adhering to the ball, and include stones not solidly embedded, leaves, twigs, branches and the like, dung, worms, and insects and casts or heaps made by them." Be aware, however, that fiddling with unstable lies is like playing a game of Pick-Up-Stix, and if the ball moves, you lose.

Nonetheless, you should try to clear away as many impediments as possible so that you can get secure footing. Most errant shots from beds of leaves and needles go astray because the golfer loses his balance on the slippery surface.

Address the ball with a square stance, and play it back an inch or so. Don't ground your club unless you want to start that chain reaction. The swing is similar to the one used for hardpan and divots. Once again, eyeball the front half of the ball, and try to catch it before you pick up any foliage, tinder, or whatever. Pull through the ball on your downswing, and don't be afraid to follow through. The flying debris won't affect your shot once you've struck the ball. Failure to follow through, on the other hand, can ruin an otherwise fine swing. So hit down *and* through.

Sandy Rough

If you play a seaside course you should know how to cope with sandy rough. "Rough" is actually a misleading term for this tight lie that has nothing to do with the bushy growths lining the fairways.

The key word in playing from sandy rough is "firm." Take a *firm* stance, a little wider than usual, with the ball slightly back of its normal position. Keep a *firm* grip on your club, because if you don't, the club may turn on contact with the hard-packed sand. In your swing, strive for that *firm* downward hit on the ball.

Shots from sandy rough should be hit carefully, with a slow, abbreviated backswing, to ensure accurate impact on the tight lie. Accordingly, take one club longer than usual. Also, don't try a wood, unless you're so confident with your woods that you'd hit one off linoleum.

The Water Blast

Most successful trouble shots are dramatic, but none is more impressive than the blast from water. Most of us have seen the pros pull off these shots on television. In a recent Masters, Ben Crenshaw hit a beauty from Rae's Creek pond on Augusta's 15th hole.

Unfortunately most explosions from water are not successful, and even the pros have their embarrassing moments. Take Bruce Devlin, who, on the 72nd hole of the 1975 San Diego Open, took six swings from the edge of a greenside pond and scored an even 10 on the hole. The mistake dropped him from 4 under to 1 over for the tournament and cost him several thousand dollars. Devlin's folly is an excellent example of poor judgment, but it also illustrates what can happen if you insist on hitting a ball in water.

Several thoughts should go through your mind before you wade into a wet lie. First, consider the Rules. There are different penalties for different types of water, and it may be to your advantage to drop out and play your shot from solid ground rather than gamble with a blast. If you're in casual water, there's no penalty at all. So be sure you know where you stand with the rulebook.

Always take a good look at your situation, not just the lie, but everything that's ahead of you. Is there a steep bank to climb? If so, the odds against you are just as steep. Does your shot have to cross a trap, or worse, more water? If it must, then think hard before you remove your shoes and socks.

Finally, what kind of lie do you have? This is the most important consideration because with water shots a basic law applies: The difficulty of extrication is directly proportional to the degree of submergence. In general, if at least half of the ball is dry you have a good chance of getting out. When all other conditions are perfect, and if you've played this shot before, you can go after a ball that's more than half covered. But if the whole ball is under water, forget it. You'll probably have enough trouble just picking it out by hand.

Normally, the best club to use for this shot is a 9-iron. The 9-iron's thin flange makes it the most effective club for slicing through the water. Of course, if you carry two wedges, the pitching wedge is your No. 1 water club.

As a general rule you shouldn't try to blast a ball out of water unless at least half of the ball is visible above the surface.

From Water: Play the ball well back, break your wrists early in the backswing, make a controlled weight shift, and hit down sharply. Your pitching wedge should penetrate the water about two inches in back of the ball. Be sure to follow through completely.

As you might imagine, balance is very important, both to the success of your shot and to your own dryness. For both reasons, keep most of your weight on your left side. Take a square stance with the ball positioned just left of center. Do not ground—in this case, water—your club, as you'll incur the same penalty you would in a sand trap.

The shot is hit similarly to an explosion from sand, with an early wrist cock on the backswing and a sharp chop down on the ball. Hit two inches behind the ball, and to guarantee that you do this, look at a spot in the water that is two inches in back of the ball. It's hard, but it's the only way. Swing with authority, and don't let up as you move into the impact area. Sure, it'll feel a bit different hitting through water, but you must finish the swing if you want to dredge the ball up and out.

A final footnote from the rulebook: If the ball should begin moving in the water, you *may* swing at it. (This is the only instance where it is permissible to hit a moving ball.) You may not, however, delay hitting the ball in order to let it drift to a more advantageous position. See Rule 25-2.

So far this chapter has dealt with shots hit from a variety of bad lies. In all of them the ball was sitting in an obviously troublesome position. Now consider this: Your ball is lying on perfectly clipped grass in the middle of the fairway. You have a wide, clear path to the green and plenty of room to take a free swing at the ball. Yet you have a bad lie.

Why?

You're on a hill.

Hilly lies come in four varieties—uphill, downhill, sidehill with the ball above your feet, and sidehill with the ball below your feet. Each of these calls for a different shot, so let's take them one at a time.

Uphill

For beginning golfers an uphill lie is often easier than a flat lie, since loft comes easily when you're hitting uphill. An uphill lie will give your shot almost automatic height, and for that reason you should use one club more than usual, unless you're very near the green. If the hill is really steep, move up two clubs—hit a 5-iron rather than a 7.

If you try to take a normal stance for an uphill shot, you'll probably feel awkward and uncomfortable. This unnatural feel-

A shot hit off an uphill lie will not go as far as one from level ground, so take one club more than you would normally hit for the distance to the pin.

ing is caused by the fact that your left side is a good bit higher than your right. The first thing to do is correct that situation. Flex your left knee a bit, lean to the left a little, and try to get your hips parallel to the slope. This will give you a more normal address position, which will facilitate solid contact with the ball.

For best contact play the ball about an inch forward of its normal position in your stance. Keep your swing easy—slower and shorter than normal—to ensure steady balance. It should be an arm-swing, with a minimum of hip and leg movement. Concentrate especially on the takeaway, in which you should glide the club down the slope. This will help you to bring it back up the slope and into the ball on your downswing.

On extra-steep slopes your shot will have a tendency to draw to the left, so compensate in these cases by aiming about five to ten yards to the right of your target.

Downhill

The downhill shot is tougher than the uphill shot, and this difficulty is again related to the relative ease—or lack of ease—of imparting loft to the shot.

In general, everything is exactly opposite to the uphill shot, beginning with club selection. Since you'll get reduced loft from a downhill lie, take one club less than you would for a level shot. Don't worry about losing distance—you're heading downhill, which automatically shortens the yardage, and, secondly, your ball will run longer than it would on flat or uphill terrain.

As with the uphill shot, the most important principle is to get your hips parallel to the slope. With downhill lies you do this by flexing your right (or uphill) knee. To be sure of getting quick loft, play the ball back an inch to two inches from its normal position in your square stance. This adjustment may seem strange, especially if you've always been taught that for maximum loft you play the ball off your left side, where you'll hit it on the upswing. But if you consider the awkwardness of the downhill lie, you'll realize that unless you play the ball back you may top it or even whiff it. To prove this, give yourself a couple of practice swings and take note of the spot where your club clips the grass. You'll see that this spot is an inch or more behind the ball position for a level shot.

Your weight should be mostly on your right side, and during the swing you should guard against shifting that weight too quickly or too greatly to the left, since you can easily lose your balance completely and stumble off the shot.

The swing itself is another of those careful, down-and-through types. Make your club follow up the slope on the three-quarter backswing and back down the hill to the ball on the downswing. Lead the club with stiff, non-rolling wrists, and more so than on any other shot, remember golf's first fundamental— keep your head down.

If the downward slope is steep, expect a few yards of left-to-right fade, and compensate by aiming left.

Sidehill With the Ball Above Your Feet

It's not hard to hit a ball from a sidehill lie when the ball is above your feet, but it's not easy to put that ball on the green.

Club selection is a little tricky. You'll have to choke up on whatever club you use, so it's wise to take plenty of stick. On the other hand, you'll probably end up hitting a draw, which will add distance, so that an extra club may not be necessary. The best formula is to let the secondary slope (uphill or downhill to the green) determine your club choice. If your sidehill lie is also heading downhill as you address the ball, hit the same club you would from a level lie. If the fairway slopes uphill, take one club more. If you are on the same altitude as the green, your club

From an Uphill Lie: Level your hips with the slope by flexing your left knee. Play the ball forward, and minimize your weight shift on the way back. Expect a mild draw, and compensate by aiming a few yards left.

When hitting from a downhill lie, take one club less than usual, since you'll need extra loft to get the ball up.

choice can go either way, though it's probably wiser to take the longer club and swing it smoothly.

Whatever club you choose, do shorten up on the grip in order to allow for the ball's being higher and therefore closer to your hands. The ball should be in its appropriate position for the club you're hitting, and you should address the ball with a square stance, your weight distributed evenly.

Your swing should be slow, steady, and no more than three-quarter length. If you swing too hard you'll likely tilt or even fall backward, and the resulting shot will be less than spectacular.

Of great importance to the success of this shot is the direction in which you aim it. From sidehill lies with the ball above your feet you'll always hit a draw, a shot that flies from right to left. Sometimes it'll be a big draw, or even a hook. So align yourself accordingly. Aim at least 20 feet to the right of your objective. That way, even if the shot hooks 40 feet you'll still be only 20 feet off the mark.

If, however, you have to hit the ball straight because trees to the near right preclude a draw, try this: For a 6-iron shot, take a 5-iron and open the face a bit at address. You'll get a nice straight shot of 6-iron height.

Sidehill With the Ball Below Your Feet

For the average golfer, the most difficult of the hilly lies, by far, is the sidehill lie with the ball below the golfer's feet. When most

From a Downhill Lie: Flex your right knee to make your hips parallel to the slope. Play the ball in the middle of your stance, and let your club follow the slope up on the take-away and down into impact. Allow for the inevitable fade by aiming 5-10 yards left.

From a Sidehill Lie with the Ball Above Your Feet: Grip down on the club at least an inch, and play for several yards of right-to-left movement on the shot. Swing well within yourself, since balance is important on this shot.

From a Sidehill Lie with the Ball Below Your Feet: Guard against the dreaded shank by taking one club extra, using a wide stance with both knees well flexed, and swinging as smoothly and carefully as possible. Aim well left of your target, because the ball will fade quite a bit.

of us approach this lie our minds have only one thought, the most menacing thought in golf—shank.

The reason most of us shank from the sidehill/downhill lie is that we tend to fall forward down the slope. In doing so we move the club out toward the ball, and the result is that we contact the ball with the inside of the clubface, often the hosel itself, instead of the sweet spot.

To avoid this fatal lean, you should make every effort to maintain an extremely firm base, an even balance, and a smooth, unhurried swing. First, take one club more than normal, because you want to give this shot that easy, unforced swing. Besides, the ball will be fading, so you'll need more stick.

Your stance should be square, with the ball in its usual position for the club you're hitting. Since balance is all-important, spread your feet out an inch or two extra. This will also help bring you down closer to the ball and thus reduce the chance that you'll top or whiff the shot. Your weight should be perceptibly back on your heels, both at address and throughout the swing.

This is one of the few swings in golf where it helps to think about your knees. Concentrate on flexing them—more than for a flat fairway shot—and keeping them flexed throughout the swing. The backswing should be a simple, slow, three-quarter move. Let your arms and hands do most of the work, and strive for smooth clean contact with the ball. Finally, if you really want to avoid that shank, keep your head down until well after impact. Again, play for the effect of the slope by aiming well left of your objective.

If you can't afford to let the ball fade in naturally, make one more adjustment. Take one less club and close the face at address. For a 6-iron distance, pull out a 7-iron and toe it in. You'll get a straight shot to the green—assuming you've followed orders with respect to the rest of the swing.

Since this lie is one of the real booby traps, you should practice these shots whenever possible. Only through practice will you gain the confidence to shut out the shanks and shoot at the pin.

This chapter has treated nearly all the natural hazards a golf course has to offer. Only one type of troublemaker has been omitted because it deserves a chapter of its own—trees.

trees

"Only God can make a tree." Perhaps that's why the name of the supreme deity is invoked so often by golfers slashing their way through the seedlings, saplings, and conifers that shade America's fairways.

When the inevitable happens and you find yourself stymied by a tree, you normally have four options: You can go under it, over it, around the right side, or around the left side. In order to do any of these things, you have to be able to "maneuver" the ball. You must know how to hit certain intentional, unconventional shots that are at the heart of every good scrambler's game.

The high shot, low shot, fade/slice, and draw/hook are all you need to learn to get your graduate degree in forest management. And even if you play most of your golf in Arabia, these four shots will improve your golf. They can help you shorten a dogleg or tame a strong wind, stop a ball quickly or make it roll endlessly. In fact, the shots in this chapter will show you the best way to deal with all trouble—to avoid it by steering clear. Learn these shots, study them, practice them, and the trees will suddenly become smaller. So will your handicap.

When hitting over trees, always take first things first. Be sure you have enough loft to clear the highest branches; then think about whether you can reach the green. Distance to the target is always the secondary consideration.

The High Shot

Occasionally each of us will hit a drive that is so bad it's good, a slice or hook so high, wide, and horrendous that it flies over everything—rough, trees, and trouble—and comes to rest in the middle of the fairway—the *wrong* fairway. As a result, we find ourselves playing a dogleg that isn't on the scorecard.

Normally, when you recover from these shots, you have to pass back over the same hazardous terrain you crossed on the previous shot, only this time you must hurdle everything in reverse order. This usually means that the trees are the first things you have to clear. Which in turn means that you had better know how to hit tree trimmer No. 1, the quick-rising high shot.

The most obvious requirement for the high shot is a lofted iron. Exactly which one to use depends primarily on two things—how close you are to the trees and how far you are from the green, with the former consideration being the more important of the two. If you need a 9-iron to clear the woods and a 5-iron to reach the green, hit the 9-iron and worry about the green on your next shot. Don't try to compromise with a 7-iron.

The key to hitting a fast-rising shot is ball position. The ball should be played well forward of its normal position in your square stance—anywhere from one to two inches, depending

The High Shot: Take a lofted iron, play the ball well forward in your stance, and swing down and through. Stay behind the ball and resist the temptation to raise up at impact.

upon how much height you need and how quickly you need it. The more height you need, the further forward you should position the ball.

Don't fiddle around with your grip or stance—you don't need to. By positioning the ball forward, you've assured yourself of catching it at the very beginning of your upward swing through the ball, thus facilitating a quickly ascending shot. Before hitting the shot, take a couple of practice swings to be sure you're clipping the grass at the right place in your stance.

In hitting the high shot—and all the other shots described in this chapter—be sure to remember the two cardinal rules of golf: Swing easy and keep your head down. Faced with these special situations, golfers have a natural tendency to hurry the swing and then look up quickly in their eagerness to see whether they've pulled off the shots. And, as we all know, fast swings and bobbing heads make for unhappy follow-throughs.

With the high shot it is especially important to stay down, since you want to make solid contact with the underside of the ball. Keep your swing smooth and compact. Hit down on the ball but don't *pull* down as you would for most hit-down shots. The left hand should not lead the way through. Both arms, in fact, should stay back, with the right hand and arm bringing the club squarely down and beneath the ball. Hit down and under, and the ball will surely go up and over.

If you find yourself having to hit one of these shots from a thick fairway lie or short rough, fear not, because the flyer characteristics of the lie will help you raise the ball. Do protect yourself against the extra grass, however, by playing the ball no more than an inch forward in your stance.

When you're just a few yards from a stand of trees and your best bet is to go over them, pull out a couple more stops. First, take your most lofted fairway club—stay away from the sand wedge—the pitching wedge is best. Next, keep the ball in a forward position, but open your stance a bit and lay open the clubface (angle it a few degrees right) for extra loft. Then go ahead and make a smooth pass at the ball. If, after doing this correctly, you still don't get over, then you can conclude with relative certainty that you chose the wrong route!

During the 1975 PGA Jack Nicklaus had one of these menacing lies on his way to victory. On Firestone Country Club's 625-yard 16th hole, a par 5 known affectionately as The Monster, Jack found himself 137 yards from the green, lieing three, and directly in back of a 30-foot tree. Using his 9-iron, he

If you think you can low-bridge the branches with a 4-iron, then hit a 3-iron. Give yourself a one-club margin of error.

rocketed the ball just over the tip of the tree and landed it on the back of the water-guarded green. From there he sank a 30-footer for the scramblingest par you'd ever want to see.

The Low Shot

When your only alternative is to go under the tree limbs, you should know how to hit the low shot.

In choosing your club remember that, as with the high shot, trajectory (in this case, the lack of it) is the prime concern, and yardage is secondary. If you're under the spreading chestnut tree, or amid several of them, you'll probably have to keep the shot low for the first 20 to 30 feet, until it gets clear of all overhanging branches. This means that, though you may be a 9-iron's distance from the green, you'd better pull out a long iron (2-, 3-, or 4-) and adjust in the following ways.

Most important, shorten up on the grip at least an inch for control. As in the high shot, ball position is important, though this time the ball should be an inch to two inches (in extreme cases, even three inches) back of its usual position in your stance. This will cause you to make contact with a clubface whose effective loft is even less than that of a 2-iron. The farther back you play the ball, the less loft your club will have at impact and the less your shot will rise.

The rearward ball position will force you to have your hands well in front of the ball at address. This is just what you want. In fact, your hands should be ahead of the club all through the swing as you hit down on it in the good old-fashioned way.

The Low Shot: Make a long, wide takeaway and a conservative backswing. After impact extend your arms straight at the target.

Begin by making a low, long takeaway, keeping the club close to the ground for at least a foot or so. Your backswing should be controlled and not too long, especially if your shot is a short one. On your downswing think only about leading through with your hands and making that clubhead come down cleanly on the ball. Try not to roll your right hand over your left at all, and keep the follow-through just as low and wide as the takeaway, with both hands pointing directly out at the target. A couple of practice swings will aid the cause and give you a good read on the precise place where you should position the ball in your stance.

You often see the pros' particular variation on this shot—the low ball that suddenly rises abruptly at an almost 45-degree angle. Arnold Palmer particularly is identified with the shot. Assuming you're not in the rough, it's not a hard shot to hit. You hit it just the same way as the low shot just described, but with one additional adjustment: Hood the club. Don't close the face, hood it, by tilting it down toward the ball a bit. The hooding will delay slightly the "take" of the backspin and thus delay the rise of the ball. Don't try this shot with any club less lofted than a 4-iron or your ball may never rise at all.

When the ceiling for your shot is extremely low—two feet or less—don't be afraid to slap the ball out with the putter. Hit the shot just as described above, but don't shorten your grip on the putter. Also, be mindful of two things: First, the shot will not work well from moderate or heavy rough. Hardpan is actually best, since the ball will scoot easily along the ground. Secondly, don't go for a lot of distance with this shot. Putters are meant for putting.

Have you ever wondered why the pros are so good? The reasons one hears on television and reads in magazines are always the same—long, straight drives, sharp chips and putts, the concentration of Buddha. But perhaps their strongest attribute is the one that's rarely mentioned: They all know how to make a golf ball bend.

Every pro on the PGA Tour can fade, slice, hook, and draw the ball intentionally. Some, of course, are better than others, and not surprisingly it is these few master shot-shapers who take home the biggest paychecks. Lee Trevino is uncannily accurate at fading and drawing. And the king of them all is Nicklaus, perhaps the only man who can change his game from fade to draw on a week's notice—and win back-to-back tournaments.

It's the same with amateurs. Good ones fade the ball on purpose and bad ones slice it by accident. The truth is that anyone who knows the basics of the golf swing can learn to make his shots do tricks. And, ironically, this ability to hit 'em crooked can go a long way toward straightening out your game.

Slices and Fades

The left-to-right shot is called either a slice or a fade, depending upon how much bend it has. While you will learn here how to hit a planned slice, the average weekend slice is completely unintentional, a severely bending eyesore that gets most golfers *into* trouble, not out of it. Its more moderate cousin, the fade, is a shot made popular and perfect by Ben Hogan and practiced widely ever since. In contrast to the slice, which even when hit intentionally is a desperate shot, the fade is normally an aggressive ploy that good golfers use to improve their accuracy.

Since confidence is one of the keynotes of this book, we'll look at the fade first and then point to the slight adjustments which can transform this controlled arc into an intentional banana ball.

The only way to fade or slice a ball is to start it off with left-to-right spin. If the ball is rotating left to right at impact, then it will move from left to right after it rises into the air.

Imparting this clockwise spin is probably the easiest thing in golf, as most unintentional slicers will attest. To hit an intentional fade, here's all you do:

1. Open your stance: Align your feet, hips, and shoulders to the left of the target line by pulling your left foot back two inches.

2. Square your clubface to your ultimate target (not to your realigned foot, hip, shoulder line).

That's it. That's all the "doctoring" you have to do to hit a controlled fade.

You see, by opening your stance you'll move your right hip out into the path of a normal square swing. This obtrusive pelvis will force you to bring the club out and away on your takeaway and bring it back down and across the ball at impact—the best way in the world to impart left-to-right spin.

Don't make any other swing adjustments. Just take a smooth, comfortable swing at the ball. If you've set up properly, your usual swing should produce that Hogan fade, one of the most useful shots in golf.

Just one note: Since the fade generally gives you more height but less distance than a normal shot, remember to take plenty of club—one or two more than for a straight shot.

When you need a big, big bender—an intentional slice—it's time for a couple of extra tricks. Here they are.

First, exaggerate the adjustment you made for the fade. Open your stance wide. Next, "weaken" your grip by rolling

Left-to-Right Shots: For a fade, simply open your stance; for a slice, open your stance and weaken your grip. For both shots, swing normally after making the pre-swing adjustments.

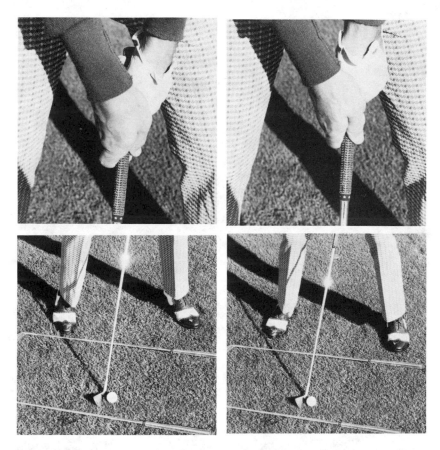

both hands to the left until the "V's" formed by your thumbs and forefingers point to your left eye. It's going to feel strange, so take a couple of swings with this new grip. No matter how unnatural it may seem, however, don't readjust to your old grip during your address and waggle.

Don't try anything fancy on the swing. As with the fade, your stance and clubhead position—now assisted by the change in grip—should prepare you for the proper cut at the ball. Just make the swing slow and smooth, with as little wristiness as possible, and keep your mind tuned in on the idea of cutting across the ball. If you can keep that in your head, and keep your head down, then you'll produce a slice the likes of which you'd normally cringe at—but this time it'll be a pleasure to watch. Remember, as with the fade, to take one or two clubs more than you would for a straight shot.

Left to right:
Slice Grip

Square Grip

Hook Grip

Left to right:
Slice Stance

Square Stance

Hook Stance

Two more thoughts on the fade and slice. First, be aware that these left-to-right shots are easier to hit with certain clubs than with others. The straight-faced clubs (driver and putter) are best because their comparatively unlofted faces produce little backspin, a force which competes with sidespin. Of course, you'll rarely pull out a driver or putter for a fairway shot, but you will be hitting lots of irons, so remember long irons fade and slice easier than short irons. Once you get into the 6- to 7-iron range, that backspin begins to assert itself and sidespin takes a back seat.

Secondly, keep in mind the fact that it's easier to slice and fade from the fairway than from the rough. Thick or wet lies reduce friction between the clubhead and ball, which inhibits your ability to put any kind of spin on the ball. So don't expect to maneuver a ball from anything but a clean dry lie. Actually,

the optimum place from which to bend a ball to the right is hardpan. The firm, bare ground allows you to make absolutely clean contact and put plenty of hard, honest left-to-right spin on the ball. So the next time you think you're in double trouble—sitting on a dirt road and stymied by a tree—fret not, because conditions are perfect for a hero shot.

Draws and Hooks

If the situation calls for a controlled right-to-left shot, your weapon is the draw. The draw is a useful shot, even if you never get into trouble with trees or obstacles. It's especially helpful on drives and long shots, since it always adds roll and distance. For this reason, you should often take one club less than you would for a normal shot.

Since you want to start the ball to the right, close your stance by aligning your hips and shoulders to the right of your target. (The ball can be in its normal position in your stance.) Square your clubface to your target.

Don't worry about your grip or swing. Your setup has brought your right hip back out of the way, and this will promote the inward takeaway and outward downswing needed for this shot. Concentrate on the basics—a smooth swing, a steady head, always keeping in mind a clear vision of the shot you want. If you know what sort of flight you want, and you make these simple stance and clubhead adjustments, you should hit a well-controlled draw. Like the fade, it pays to practice this shot so that you can zero in on the exact set-up that draws the ball most effectively and consistently for you.

When you need a big, roundhouse hook to get you back in the ballgame, try a couple of extra amendments to your address.

Accentuate the stance alteration required for the draw by closing your stance another inch. Also, change your grip by rolling your hands to the right until the "V's" formed by your thumbs and forefingers point toward your right pants pocket. Don't make any deliberate physical changes in the swing, except to swing as slowly as possible. Think about hitting out toward

Right-to-Left Shots: For a draw, simply close your stance; for a hook, close your stance and strengthen your grip. For both shots, swing naturally after making the pre-swing adjustments.

the right, and keep that vision of your ideal shot clearly in mind. The chances are good that you'll hit it.

Since a hook shot means extra roll and run, more even than a draw, hit one club less than for a draw, or two clubs less than for a straight ball. If you'd hit a 3-iron directly at the green, then take a 5-iron when you're playing an intentional hook. If the path is uphill, however, go with a 4-iron.

Also, as with all bending shots, the hook is a hard thing to produce from a lie in the rough. So don't expect any 45-degree-angle miracles when you have a thick lie.

Finally, keep one important concept in mind when hitting all left-to-right and right-to-left shots. If you have a natural tendency to hit hooks, you'll need extra "doctoring" with your setup and grip to hit intentional fades and slices. The same is true if you're a natural slicer and want to draw and hook. You'll have to try a little harder.

You should also be able to use the principles outlined here to straighten your tee and fairway shots. If you've been slicing, whether for five holes or five years, you can generally straighten things out by applying and practicing the intentional hook adjustments just discussed. Likewise, the prescription for an intentional slice can be an excellent remedy for a chronic case of the right-to-left bends.

A solid knowledge of the intentional shots can help you out of all sorts of predicaments. If your ball lies a foot from a brick wall and you have to hit in the direction of ten o'clock, an intentional hook can be very useful. In stiff headwinds a low shot can give you a big edge over your opponents.

By combining techniques for two intentional shots you can create a third shot, which will accomplish something that neither of the individual shots could. Suppose, for instance, that you need an 8-iron to clear the top of a tree but a 7-iron to reach the green. Your answer, if you know how to hit both the high shot and the draw, is to hit a high, drawing 8-iron. Just set up for the hook, with a closed stance, and adjust for the high shot by playing the ball forward of its normal position in your stance. The extra distance of the draw will get you home. This is just one of several hybrid shots that are available to you if you know how to hit the "big six"—the high shot, low shot, fade, slice, draw, and hook.

A Last Resort

This chapter began by noting there are just four ways to bypass a

When there's absolutely no other way, choose the largest opening that allows you a shot to the green, then punch the ball to daylight.

tree—over, under, around the left, and around the right. That statement is not strictly true, because a fifth alternative does exist. However, this final way is truly a last resort, and that's why it has been saved until now.

Your last option is to go *through* the tree. Yes, through it. And why not? There are times when slamming one through the leaves and limbs is actually the most intelligent route to follow. The whole trick is identifying these occasions when a desperation shot is necessary.

Playing through a tree or group of trees is recommended when all of the following things are true:

1. All other avenues—over, under, and around—are impossible. Not just doubtful, impossible.

2. An unplayable lie will not help you, because . . .

3. You are in a tight match, with no room to lose a hole. Your opponent is in good shape, so you have to make your next shot a good one.

Here's an example. It's the 18th hole, a par 4, and your match is all even. Your opponent is ten feet from the pin in two, and you lie two in the woods, just in back of the green. A large trap guards the back of the green, so you can't play a low, running punch shot. You can't declare an unplayable lie and take a penalty shot because this would mean you'd have to sink your next shot in order to have any chance of keeping the match alive. Your only alternative is to axe out through the trees and hope for the best. If you think this sounds like an Arnold Palmer shot, you're right. In fact, Arnie credits his first British Open victory at

Royal Birkdale in 1961 to a "clincher" he punched through a patch of willow scrub.

Since these shots are rarely played, there's no traditional method to follow. Basically, you have to adapt to each crisis, and use both your common sense and imagination to solve the problem. This is the way all good trouble shots begin.

Normally you'll have at least two alternatives. We'll call the first of these the "pick-and-punch" method. You pick the airiest, least dense spot in the trees that's in line with your objective, and, using an iron of appropriate loft, you punch the ball out through the opening with a stiff-wristed shot. If the clearing is left of your line to the green, open your clubface and cut-punch the ball with an outside-in chop at impact. If it's to the right, close your clubface, roll your wrists as you come into the ball, and hope for the best.

When there are two openings or airy spots—a small one directly in line with the pin and a large one in line with the green but not the pin, hit for the large one. This way you'll have a good chance of getting out of the woods and a fair chance of getting close, which is better than having a fair chance of getting out in the first place. Even in these desperate situations, you should view your nearest hurdle as the most important one. Never get too far ahead of yourself.

Sometimes, of course, there are no openings anywhere. This is when you should try the second option of your last resort—go ahead and rifle one through the leaves and branches.

The trick here is to estimate the amount of resistance the tree will offer and to hit your shot with enough force so that, after being slowed down, it will continue far enough to reach the green. This will, of course, be a guess, and the only way to prepare for such shots is to take fifteen minutes someday and hit a couple of dozen balls through the trees. A little practice, in this instance, will go a long way.

The through-the-trees shot may be a low-percentage shot, but it is nonetheless a shot, a legitimate shot, and under certain circumstances, the most intelligent shot. If planned correctly and played with confidence it can bring big surprises to both you and your opponent. Put one of these shots up close and it's a safe bet that you'll win the hole. Your opponent will be so rattled that he'll 3-putt from 10 feet and yield to your scrambling par.

trick shots

During an 18-hole round of golf, the average player, say a 15-handicapper, will have a minimum of 54 perfect lies—one on every tee and two on every green—assuming he takes 36 putts. In addition, Mr. Average will play nearly three dozen shots off an assortment of lies ranging in quality from very good (fairway and fringe) to poor (heavy rough, traps, steep hills). Finally, in the course of that round he will probably make himself the victim of at least one real stinker, a lie so wicked and uncooperative that it defies categorization, at least in polite language.

If he deserves his 15, Mr. Average will take fair advantage of most of his good lies and make the best of most of his bad ones. But when he gets to that one death trap, anything will be possible. At best he'll declare the lie unplayable, take a one-stroke penalty, and try to drop the ball in position for a recovery shot. Unfortunately, this option guarantees him nothing more than an extra stroke on the scorecard, and if handled improperly it can lead to a predicament far worse than the one from which it originated.

Frequently a fearless 15 will try to swing his way out of jail but will make one of two mistakes. Either he'll choose the wrong way out or he'll choose the right way but mishit his shot. Whether the error is mental or physical the consequences are the same: rising of blood pressure and score, followed by loss of composure and/or ball and/or match. Very often, it is the inability to deal with these backbreaker lies that prevents the 15-handicapper from ever becoming a 10.

The Left-Handed Shot

If one trick shot is recognized and accepted widely today, it is the left-handed shot. During the last two decades, television has enabled us to watch the touring pros scramble with these shots from the opposite side of the ball. We have thus seen that the lefty shot not only exists—it works.

Success with the left-handed shot needn't be restricted to the pros, because it isn't as difficult as it sounds. Like many of the shots in this chapter, the key is knowing not *how* but *when* to hit it.

When should you try a left-handed shot? Quite simply, when you can't hit a right-handed shot, when your ball lies so close to an obstacle that you can't take a stance and swing from the conventional side.

There are at least two schools of thought on how to play the shot. The difference of opinion centers on the question of which side of the clubface should contact the ball. One group recommends turning the club toe-down and hitting with the usual scored face. The other advocates flipping the club around and hitting the ball with the chromed brand-name side of the club.

There is room in the scrambler's game for both methods. If you need a certain amount of loft and distance you should probably go with the first technique, the upside-down clubface. A 7-iron, which combines a reasonably large face with a good amount of loft, is your best club.

If, on the other hand, you're near the green and can skittle the ball at the hole, or if overhanging branches prohibit a lofted shot, then it would be safer and simpler for you to hit the ball with the back of your club. A 2-iron should be your choice for this one, since it has the straightest back of any of the clubs. Of course, if you have a blade putter, by all means use it. This will be the one time it can give you more loft and distance than any other club in the bag.

Top left
Lefty Shot # 1: Use a 7-iron, reverse your grip, and hit the ball with toe of the clubface.

Top right
Lefty Shot # 2: Use a 2-iron, reverse your grip, and hit the ball with the brand-name side of the club.

Left
Why stand in the trap and choke up to the steel of your club when you can comfortably backhand a putt at the pin?

Regardless of which clubhead position you choose, be sure to reverse your hand positions, gripping the club with your right hand higher than your left. As far as the rest of the swing is concerned, don't try to do everything in reverse. Just remember that with a lefty shot you must keep your right arm, not your left, straight. Don't take any more than a half-swing at the ball. Of course, no matter on which side of the ball you're standing, it's important to *swing easy and keep your head down.*

Practice this one a few times and you'll be surprised at how adept you can be. If you'd like inspiration consider Harry Vardon, golf's most renowned switch-hitter. He could shoot par from either side of the ball!

The One-Handed Chop

If you want an alternative to the lefty shot—a very good alternative—consider the one-handed chop. This one, hit with only your right arm, may look strange, but it's extremely easy to play, and you can get plenty of distance out of it.

Stand with your back to your target and position yourself so that the ball is about five inches directly to the right of your right foot. Taking a 9-iron or wedge, square the club to your intended line of flight and choke down to the middle of the grip. Then just go ahead and take a straight, pendulumlike chop. For short shots and chips, stiff-arm the shot, with no wrist action. When you want distance, cock your wrist and take a full swing. Don't be surprised if you hit the ball almost as far with one hand as with two!

The Between-the-Legs Shot

Ever tried a between-the-legs shot? Probably not, but chances are you should have at some point in your golfing life. This one can be a real lifesaver when your normal takeaway is blocked.

The between-the-legs shot should never be played with anything less lofted than a 9-iron. A pitching wedge is the optimum club. Take a wider-than-normal stance, with your feet parted at a distance greater than the width of your shoulders. Stand so that your back is to your objective. The ball should be an inch or so farther away from you than usual and should be dead center in your stance.

Turn your club so that the face is square to your target line, straight through your legs. The swing is not really a swing—it's a chop. Just lift the clubhead straight up and return it to the back of the ball. At least with this shot you don't have to worry about a follow-through. Give the ball a deliberate downward blow. Take a couple of practice chops before you try this one, because it's important that you make sharp, clean contact with the ball. If your axe swing brings the club down the least bit behind the ball, you'll just embed the club in the ground. If you come down on top of the ball, you'll just hammer it into the turf, so be sure your setup and swing are right before you take the chop that counts. If you chop properly, the ball will pop up and scoot between your legs. It will take one quick bounce and then roll like a chip shot hit with a 2-iron. On hard ground, this shot may be hit with a putter.

The One-Handed Chop: Stand with your back to your target, and grip down on the club. Stiff-arm the short shots, and break your wrists when you want more distance.

The Between-the-Legs Shot: Use a pitching wedge, take a wide stance, and chop down to the back of the ball.

Incidentally, don't worry about hitting yourself in the groin. Your unorthodox stance has reduced the effective loft on that 9-iron or wedge to a point where its angle at impact will be equal to that of a 1-iron. And, as most of us know, there is no way you can make a 1-iron rise up one foot before it has traveled two feet. So don't worry about causing distress in the lower tract as a result of this shot.

The Reverse-Croquet Shot: A variation of the between-the-legs shot, this one allows you to put more loft on the ball by using your left hand as a hinge.

Don't be afraid to grip well down on the club if it will give you better leverage.

The Reverse-Croquet Shot

A variation of the between-the-legs shot is a maneuver we'll call the reverse-croquet shot. This one is also useful when you have little room to stand or swing in the conventional way. The difference in the between-the-legs shot and the reverse-croquet shots is that the latter allows you to actually follow through between your legs. You won't get as much power as you would from the between-the-legs shot, since you'll be chipping instead of chopping. However, you'll gain a couple of things which can be more important—loft and touch. Here's how.

Once again, grab a lofted club—anywhere from a 7-iron to a wedge—and face the ball, taking a wide stance with your back to your target. This time, cosy up to the ball; stand at least as close to it as you would when putting (or playing croquet). In fact, if your backswing is really cramped, feel free to stand *directly over the ball* so that it is smack between your feet. The closer you stand to the ball, the more loft you'll be able to put on it.

Now for the important part—the grip. Both the left- and the right-hand grips are unorthodox, even outlandish. With your left hand, grab the handle so that your thumb hooks over the tip of the shaft. Your hold on the club should resemble the grip you take on a pop bottle when you want to fizz it up—if you still do such things. In this position, the left hand will act as a hinge throughout the swing.

Slide your right hand down to a point several inches south of the grip, and hold the club with your thumb, index finger, and forefinger, much the same way you'd grip a large pen. Be sure the clubface is square to your target, with the toe-end touching the ground.

To hit the shot, simply lead the club back and up with your right hand and then bring it back through. (This is one swing where you should have no trouble keeping your clubhead square to the ball throughout the swing.) Make your backswing as lengthy as permitted, and strive for a full follow-through. As always, stay down by maintaining a wide base and a steady head.

Practice this one around the putting green sometime (when no one's looking). You'll be astounded at how comfortable it is, and how accurately you can chip when you have your back to the hole!

The Restricted-Backswing Shot

Now let's suppose you have a lie which allows you to stand up to the ball from the correct side, and permits a takeaway but does not leave you room for a full backswing. Low-hanging branches prohibit a full lift of the club. What do you do?

One solution might be to hit an intentional hook, as described in Chapter 4. The flatter inside plane of the hook swing might be low enough to get under the branches. But if your situation precludes this possibility, you can always try a restricted-backswing shot.

This shot involves nothing more than curtailing your takeaway/backswing to fit the confines of your situation, and getting the greatest possible power from this abbreviated swing.

First, select the club you feel will best get the job done. Remember that your prime consideration is to get out of trouble, and the second is to get to the cup. If you know you can accomplish both things in one shot, fine, but if you have any doubts, concentrate on getting out of jail and into the clear. If this means having to hit an 8-iron instead of a 3-iron, sobeit.

Whatever club you choose, shorten your grip in order to get better control (go right down to the metal or even the clubhead if that gives you comfortable leverage). Also, stand a bit closer to the ball to compensate for the shortened grip. Swing the club with little leg or body movement, but plenty of wrist action.

The No-Backswing Shot: Address the ball from a top-of-the-backswing position with your wrists fully cocked. Then, keeping a steady head, pull down through the shot with your hands.

Break your wrists almost immediately at the start of the take-away, and snap them back quickly at the start of the downswing. These actions will pack maximum power into your constricted swing. And although it may not seem likely, you can get excellent distance and direction from this shot. It's logical, after all. How many times have you been told that the key to power and accuracy is a compact, controlled backswing?

The No-Backswing Shot

Let's take another problem. Suppose you have a full swing at the ball but one little thin branch or stalk cuts into the plan of your backswing. It's not enough to impede your swinging, but it's so disconcerting that you can't keep your mind on the shot. This one overhanging twig can be such a mental chigger that a backswing is impossible. Your answer? Skip the backswing altogether and start your swing from the top.

Sound crazy? Maybe it is, but if it works, who cares? You may be surprised to learn that there are several good golfers who *never* use backswings, and that there are touring pros (Johnny Miller is one) who advocate the no-backswing method as a learning and practice tool.

Look at it this way: Most swing mistakes occur in the backswing, so by eliminating the backswing you decrease your margin of swing error. Also, since 100 percent of your power originates at the beginning of the downswing, there is little reason to start any earlier.

To hit this no-backswing shot, just address the ball from a

top-of-the-backswing position with your wrists fully cocked. The smoothest way to reach this stance, of course, is to backswing into it. But once you get to the top, freeze, as you would over a putt. Then, keeping your eye on the ball, just pull down and through with your hands. Swinging down from this position, you'll swish right past the stalk or twig and through to your ball.

The no-backswing shot can also be useful in those restricted-backswing situations. Simply start the downswing from the point where the obstacle blocks your backswing. A general caution, however, before you try the no-backswing shot: Give it a few dry runs. Since this is such an unorthodox maneuver, you should get used to it before unveiling it during a serious round of golf.

The Kneeling Shot

Now let's assume you're really in deep trouble. Your ball is sitting at the base of a big bush. The thick upper branches prohibit a shot—a least a standing shot. But the base is well within your reach and you have an opening through the bush to the green. Prescription? The kneeling shot.

The kneeler is one of several strange and amusing shots hit with great panache and effectiveness by the late Paul Hahn, the trick-shot master of all time. Hahn claims that while hitting shots from his knees he has twice lipped the cup from 200 yards out. If he can do that well, you can certainly bat your way out from under a bush.

Since the kneeling shot, like most others in this chapter, is completely unconventional, you needn't worry about making a classic swing. It's just a matter of adapting your movements to the branches and the ball. However, do keep a couple of things in mind.

First, take a reasonably lofted club (7-iron to wedge). The wide face of the low irons will give you plenty of hitting surface with which to meet the ball. Don't worry about hitting it too high and catching the branches; your stance (if it can be called that in this case) will cause the club to be much less lofted than normal when it comes into the ball. In fact, the club will have not loft but hook at impact. For this reason, aim a bit to the right.

As you might guess, the swing is mostly arms and hands. Give it a good wristy pass, releasing your hands in a firm slap at the ball. Take a few quick practice swings to the back of the ball and up and back. For once, you don't have to worry about

The Kneeling Shot: Take a lofted iron and make a short but wristy swing through the ball. You'll hook this one, so aim well left.

staying down on the ball, but do keep still and firm. Swing slowly and steadily and you'll be off your knees and on the green in no time.

The Slap Shot

If someone asked you which sport has a "slap shot," you'd probably say hockey, and you'd be right. But here's a slap shot for scrambling golfers. However, it's not the ball that you slap, it's the club.

Let's suppose you're lying just off the green but your ball is sitting three inches in front of a big, gnarled, knotty root. In short, there's no way you can swing at it. Don't despair. You can keep the club stationary and slap the shaft so that it swings through and hits the ball.

The Slap Shot: Position the club behind the ball. Then, while holding on
loosely with your left hand, slap the
lower part of the shaft with your
right hand.

Hold the club firmly with your usual left-hand grip and
position it about a half-inch behind the ball. Now bend down and
give the lower part of the shaft a sharp slap. Go ahead and slap
the steel with your open palm. You'll get quite a few feet out of
this shot, and that's often all you need. In any case, it's usually
better than the giant step sideward you'd take by declaring an
unplayable lie.

Incidentally, lest you think this shot is illegal, refer to decision 52-101 on Rule 19-1 in the Decisions Book on the USGA
Rules of Golf. Unconventional, yes; illegal, no.

The Intentional Fat Shot

Imagine yourself in this predicament. You're just 20 feet from
the pin, but 12 of that 20 feet is taken up by a sand trap. The pin
is cut close to the edge of the green, just on the other side of the
trap, and you have to get the ball close if you want to stay alive
in your match. To make things worse, your lie is tight. It's early
morning and the grass has just been cut, so you can't get your
wedge underneath the ball to hit a high cut shot. What do you
do? Simple—you hit the shot fat, intentionally fat.

Most of us have hit this shot so often (by accident) that it
should come easy. However, it's a little tricky when you actually
are *trying* to do it. The key is to hit it like a sand shot. Address a
point in the grass about two inches behind the ball. Align yourself
so that point is midway in your slightly open stance. Close the
face of your pitching wedge, and then just hit an explosion
shot. Take a short, wristy backswing, and drive your club down
into the dirt. Naturally, this shot will work only when the ground

The Intentional Fat Shot: Address a point two inches in back of the ball, keep your eye on that spot as you swing, and hit down on it hard to explode the ball as you would from a bunker.

is reasonably moist. It's great for getting out of plugged lies, but don't try it on hard terrain unless you want a broken club and/or a broken arm. Also practice this one a couple times before you try it for real. Such practice will not only help you hit this shot, it will show you what you've been doing wrong on those fat wedges you've been hitting.

The Carom Shot

There is at least one more shot to consider when your ball is sitting near a wall and you want to hit directly back and away from the wall—the carom shot.

Naturally, this shot involves a certain amount of guesswork with regard to the angle of carom and the amount of force to use. But even a badly guessed shot will probably stand you in better stead than taking an unplayable-lie penalty.

A couple of points of commonsense advice: First, always check to see whether you're entitled to relief under the rules. The wall may be an immovable obstruction, in which case you'll be able to take a free drop. Secondly, don't expect too much distance or accuracy unless you have a smooth wall and plenty of swinging room. If the barrier is made of smooth concrete, you have a much better chance than if it's brick or craggy rock. Thirdly, try not to aim your carom so that it hits you on the return bounce. Plan this shot carefully, and you can turn a potentially disastrous situation into a triumph.

During the final round of the 1972 Westchester Classic, Gay Brewer hit a particularly daring variation of the carom shot.

The Carom Shot: Be sure the surface is smooth and hard, then just hit the ball as you normally would, only a bit harder. Stay down through the shot, and be careful not to hit yourself with the carom.

Brewer's second shot to the par-4 fifth hole had come to rest directly at the foot of a huge tree that bordered the green. He had no more than 30 feet of slightly downhill surface to the cup, but he couldn't get his club between the ball and the tree.

Brewer pondered his predicament for several minutes as the large gallery murmured speculatively over his fate. Then suddenly he addressed the ball *facing the tree*. Using a low-lofted iron, he actually chipped the ball up the sloping trunk of the tree. It climbed nearly two feet, then rolled back down across the fringe and onto the green, finishing about two feet from the cup. Brewer went on to make his par, and while he didn't win the tournament, he hit what was easily the most inventive shot of the week, a model of scrambling savoir faire.

The Vibration Shot: Address the stake, or whatever it is you're forced to hit in order to "send" the ball. Then just give it a good sharp rap. Don't swing at this one *too* hard, however, if you value your wrists.

The Vibration Shot

Now suppose that your ball ends up at the base of an out-of-bounds stake, actually leaning against the stake so that you can't get your club on the ball. As you should know, you may not move O-B markers. And you can't very well roll the ball up the stake as Brewer did with the tree. There is a shot, however, that can get you as much as 100 yards.

The answer is to hit the *stake* and let the vibrations of the wood transmit to the ball and pop it out. This shot is just like "sending" in croquet, and while it may not be the best thing in the world for your club, it could save you a match some day. What's more, it's perfectly legal.

Just address the stake (it's okay to take your stance out of bounds) and give it a good rap (with your least favorite club). Just be careful not to break (literally) your wrists. You'll be surprised at the yardage this shot will get you. In fact, it pays to use a little finesse and a half-swing, if you don't have far to go.

The Putter Poke

As already noted, the trusty putter can come in handy where other clubs are worthless. The blade putter is unique in that you can hit shots with three sides of it: low running shots with the normal face, left-handed shots with the backhand side, and *pokes* with the toe.

The poke shot is useful when your ball wanders into a narrow rut or ditch formed by erosion. If the area isn't ground under repair, you have to get the ball out in one way or another, and there's no reason to pick it out with your hand if you can force it out with your putter. By addressing the ball with the toe of the putter and taking a short, pendulumlike swing you can pop your way out of a tight lie where other clubs just won't fit.

The Rules of golf impose very few restrictions on the way a golfer may strike the ball. They say only that the ball may not be "pushed, scraped, or spooned" and that you must not hit the ball twice with one swing. The one restriction on the stance is that you may not build it up (i.e., you can't move a bench under a tree in order to hit a ball perched in high branches). On the green you may not stand astride your putting line. Within these few limitations you may grip the club, stand up to the ball, and swing at it in any way you find comfortable and convenient.

Since the Rules don't inhibit you, don't limit yourself with a closed mind. The real trick to trick shots is using your imagination and ingenuity to solve the unusual problems that are part of every round of golf. The shots presented here are just a few of the more common inventions. There are dozens more, as numerous and varied as the situations which demand them, and they all lie ready in the minds of scrambling golfers.

6.

greenside finesse

Among the major golf championships of the recent past none was more dramatic than Lee Trevino's stunning victory in the 1972 British Open. Thwarting Jack Nicklaus's bid that year for the third leg of golf's modern grand slam, Trevino awed the Muirfield gallery and millions of television viewers with a short game that bordered on the incredible.

During the last two rounds of the championship, Trevino's wedge was like a magic wand, plucking the ball from heather-lined potholes, steep bunkers, and greenside rough, and making it materialize close to—and occasionally *in*—the cup. Lee later observed that, over the final 36 holes, his shot-making around the green saved him six strokes—just enough to give him a one-shot victory over Jack.

Trevino's triumph illustrates what is perhaps the preeminent truth of twentieth-century golf: The difference between first place and the rest of the pack is a well-oiled short game. The winners of tournament after tournament, when asked about their key to success, point to a hot week around the greens. The pros simply can't survive without a strong wedge and putter.

Yet, as vital as a good short game is to the professional, it is more important to amateurs—not in terms of a livelihood but as a way toward lower scores and better golf.

The amateur's comparatively inconsistent iron game forces him to hit a great number of third and fourth shots from around the green—far more of these shots than pros hit. Pros hit irons *onto* greens, amateurs hit *near* them.

The weekend golfer with a good short game will often save pars and sometimes make birdies. The guy who can't get up and down will put lots of sixes on his card. For that reason alone the short game should be the first practice priority for any amateur. Sadly, it's usually last.

Everyone likes to boom the teeshots and slap the 5-irons from the practice tee, but few golfers spend much time around the practice green. *On* the green, yes, but around the green, huh-uh. This is a shame, not only because the short game is so important but because it's so easy to sharpen if you give it half a try.

Only pros and top amateurs are capable of hitting long and straight drives and fairway shots, but anyone can build a good short game. No power is needed—just accuracy, and that can be learned from books such as this one and refined through practice. With practice you'll develop consistency, with consistency confidence, and with confidence you'll suddenly gain the greenside finesse that is the soul of scrambling golf.

The Full Wedge

The longest of the short shots is the full wedge. "Full" should not be misunderstood to mean "hard," because no wedge should ever be hit with a strong, forceful swing..Though firm, the wedge swing is smooth, and shorter than that of any other iron.

Address the ball with an open stance and your weight about 60 percent on your left side. Keep the clubface square and stand so that the ball is just right of your left heel.

Don't make any conscious changes in your grip or swing. Just think about swinging down firmly and hitting the ball with

The Full Wedge: Ball position is in the middle of the open stance. The backswing begins with an early wrist break, is relatively inactive in the legs, and never extends beyond the three-quarter length. Swing down confidently, and hit the ball with your upper body, mostly with your right hand. Don't forget to follow through fully.

the arms and hands, especially your right hand. Probably the cause of most poor wedge shots is a reluctant, hesitant downswing, followed by a collapse of the hands at impact. So keep your right hand from rolling over the left as you come into the ball, and in the follow-through point both hands toward the pin. If all goes well, that's where your ball will be heading.

When hitting a short shot, whether it's a 100-yard wedge or a 10-foot chip, remember that everything should be done in moderation. The swing should be slow and smooth, and the club should not be brought back too far. Even on the full wedge your hands should not rise any farther than just above your shoulders. Body movement should also be minimized, with a limited hip turn and a left heel that is planted firmly throughout the swing. Above all, keep your head quiet. The less your head moves, the less chance your ball will have of deviating from the intended path.

The Fading Wedge

It's useful to be able to hit a variety of wedge shots. The first of these is the fade mentioned in Chapter 4, a left-to-right shot that floats high and settles quickly. For courses with hard, trap-guarded greens or stiff winds, the fading wedge is a very handy shot.

This shot is addressed nearly identically to the full wedge, except that you should aim it about 10-15 feet farther left. Be sure your hips and shoulders are open and that the leading edge of your wedge is square to your target. For extra height, play the ball off your left instep.

The secret to fading this short shot is in taking the club back on a markedly outside path. (With the longer clubs, you normally don't need to strain to produce this outside-in swing, but with the wedge you must be sure to put enough sidespin on the ball to overcome the backspin inherent in shots hit with such a lofted club. Otherwise, the backspin will control the shot completely and the ball won't fade at all.) So take the club away well outside the normal line.

Use the same controlled swing you use for a full wedge, and as you come into the ball, think of hitting under and across it. You'll get this feeling if you're careful not to let your hands roll over. The hands should feel, in fact, as if they're almost rolling *under* at impact, imparting that left-to-right spin.

This is a tough shot, and you'll probably have trouble with

it the first few times. You may top it; you may even shank it; but if you keep practicing it, it will come.

The Half Wedge

The half wedge, producing a ball that travels 10-15 yards less than a full wedge, is a shot that every scrambler should master.

Misunderstanding obscures the relative simplicity of this shot. Many fine amateur golfers assume that in order to produce a half wedge they must swing with half the power they would use for a full wedge. Consequently they change the comfortable tempo of their usual swing, often "quit" on the shot, and seldom put the ball where they want it to go.

A half wedge—or half shot of any kind, for that matter—is *not* based on a swing of 50-percent power. It is not a light swing—just a short one. Everything is a bit smaller.

Shorten your grip at least an inch and, in taking your open stance, position your feet an inch or so closer together than for a full wedge. The ball should be opposite your left heel. Keeping your wrists firm, take a smooth backswing which should be three-quarters that of a full wedge. At the top of the backswing your hands should be about the same height they'd be if you were ready to swing a baseball bat.

Accelerate as you normally would on the downswing, but don't be afraid to follow through. The finish of the swing is very important, and you should never quit on it.

In short, abbreviate everything—grip length, stance, pivot, wrist-break—but be firm throughout the swing. The best way to determine your own range with these "part shots" is to practice them hard and often, making appropriate adjustments until you can tailor your swing to the distance you need, hitting not only half wedges but three-quarter wedges, seven-eighth wedges, and maybe even fifteen-sixteenth wedges.

The Punch Shot

If you play on a course such as Pebble Beach, where the normal playing conditions include a 20-m.p.h. gale, you had better know how to hit a punch shot. The low-boring trajectory of the punch makes it a lifesaver in all types of heavy winds. And even when the air is still, this shot can help you out of an occasional jam.

Though the punch can be hit with the pitching wedge, a 9-iron is a wiser choice. The reduced loft of the 9 will decrease your angle of trajectory and so increase your control, especially

in a wind. Keep in mind, however, that you'll often be hitting a shot of 50-100 yards, so a couple of the half-swing adjustments will be necessary.

Choke up about an inch on the club, and take a slightly open stance with the ball between your feet. Your hands should be well in front of the ball and at least 70 percent of your weight should be on your left side. This address setup, with the club square but naturally hooded, is the exact position you want to have at impact.

Keeping your wrists absolutely stiff, take a short "baseball"-height backswing, with very little pivot or transfer of weight. Then lean back into the ball with your arms and legs, returning your weight rapidly to the left side. Stay firm-wristed through impact, and don't allow that right hand to roll over and close the clubface unless you want to pull the ball way left. Make your follow-through low, and extend your arms so that the club points straight at the flag.

The Pitch Shot

The pitch shot is a high, lofting shot that generally stops soon after it hits the green. Hit from distances of 10-80 yards, it is especially useful for clearing traps, water, and other hazards. There are as many variations on the pitch as there are golfing situations, but they're all based on the same technique.

Most pitch shots should be hit with the pitching wedge. If you don't have one, get one, because the 9-iron won't do, and neither will the sand wedge. The pitching wedge (or 10-iron) hits a wide spectrum of shots that the 9-iron and sand wedge together can't cover properly. For $20 (less if you buy it secondhand) you'll be well armed for most contingencies around the green.

To hit the basic pitch, grip the wedge as you would any other club, but shorten up about an inch. Square your clubface to the ball and assume a slightly narrow, well-open (40 degrees) stance with the ball positioned just back of your left heel. This should set you up so that your left arm is a straight extension of the club. Over half your weight should be left, and your knees

---

The Punch Shot: Using a 9-iron or pitching wedge, position the ball well back in your slightly open stance. Nearly three-quarters of your weight will be on your left side. Make an unforced swing with little pivot. Stay firm-wristed into the ball, and extend out low, never allowing your right hand to roll over your left.

The Basic Pitch: Grip down an inch on your pitching wedge, and take an open stance, with your knees well flexed and your nose just back of the ball. Since accuracy, not power, is the key, use a controlled swing, with little leg or wrist action on the way back. Hit down crisply and stay down through the ball.

When you must hit a high shot to a tight pin placement, the cut shot is the answer.

should be flexed so that you stay down on the ball even though you're gripping down on a short-shafted club.

The swing is mostly a hands-and-arms proposition. Don't use much wrist action, as overly flippy wrists can throw off your shot's alignment very quickly. Pivot and hip movement should be minimized, too. Since accuracy, not distance, is the key, you want to keep your head as still as possible. One way to do this is to plant your left foot firmly at address and keep it planted throughout the backswing, downswing, and follow-through. The backswing should probably not be longer than half-way back, but it will vary slightly according to the distance you have to cover. Since you'll normally need both height and backspin from a pitch, you should strive for that crisp, downward blow essential to backspin shots. The best way to ensure this is to lead the downswing with your hands, pulling down and through the ball.

Take a couple of quick practice swings to be certain that the back of your left hand is square to the target at impact and has not rolled under. If the left hand is square your shot will be on the money nine times out of ten. Finally, above all, stay down on the shot. There's a tremendous temptation to take a peek—to look up early—on the pitch shots. If you should peek, you won't like what you'll see, so stay down. The well-hit shot is worth that extra minisecond of waiting.

The Cut Shot

Suppose you need height quickly and backspin just as quickly. You have a good lie (not bare or tight) and you're about 25 feet from the stick, but midway between you and your goal is a 10-foot hedge. Your only alternative, if you want to put the ball close, is to hit a cut shot over the hedge.

This variation of the pitch is *not* an easy shot to hit. What's more, if you mishit it by just a bit you'll pay heavily, with a skull, a shank, or a fat shot. However, with lots of practice you can learn to hit this shot consistently, and when you do, you'll see just how useful it is.

Mastering the cut shot can have greater benefits than an occasional scrambling par. The cut is probably the epitome of golfing finesse, so when you drop the ball next to the pin from a seemingly impossible situation, you can derive a psychological boost or deliver an unexpected blow to your opponent. In short, the cut shot is well worth whatever amount of practice it takes to learn it.

The Cut Shot: A wide-open stance, an open clubface, and a rearward ball position will set you up for the outside, markedly upward takeaway and the descending cut across the ball. If you hit the shot properly the ball will settle soon after it hits the green.

The principle involved in hitting the cut is the same as that for the intentional slice. Essentially, you aim your body left, your clubface right, and swing outside-in to put left-to-right spin on the ball. When you do all this to drive or hit an iron, the ball will make a big bend from left to right. On a shot such as the cut, however, the ball is rarely struck hard enough to slice. The effects, instead, are increased height (from the open face) and lots of backspin and stop (from the cutting action).

Take your wedge (a sand wedge is often better for this shot) and address the ball with a wide-open stance—legs, hips, and shoulders are facing well left. Your left foot should be opened so that your toe is pointing just right of the pin. Since on a flat green the left-to-right spin of your shot will cause your ball to bounce a bit to the right, compensate by aiming a couple of feet left of the flagstick.

Your clubface should be laid flat back and open—aimed 15-20 degrees right of your target. Play the ball off your left toe so that your hands are just in back of the ball. This will add to the effective loft on the clubface. Weaken your grip by sliding your hands a quarter-turn counterclockwise. This grip position will guard against a wrist-roll at impact, which would close the clubface and ruin the shot.

Several practice swings are in order. Use an outside and upward takeaway, breaking your wrists early. Since you must make very accurate contact with the ball, keep the swing "quiet," with little pivot or weight shift and a short, controlled back-swing. On the downswing, concentrate on slipping the club across and under the ball. Don't try to scoop it up. If you hit this shot properly, the ball will sit soon after it hits the green. When hit from the fairway, it will also hop right on its first bounce, so take this into account when you set up, by aiming a foot or two left.

Once again, practice this shot a lot. It's great fun to hit cut shots in your backyard, even if you use plastic practice balls. Try to see how close you can stand to a bush or a clothesline, or your car, and still cut the ball up and over it. When you can clear your car from three feet away, you've mastered the cut shot.

The Lob

Now suppose you're still behind that hedge, but the pin is way in the back of the green. You want to get the ball up and then make it run and roll to the cup.

You *could* play a hard, long cut shot, but you'd be safer hitting a lob. The golf lob is similar to the overspin lob in tennis, a lazy, arching shot that bounces forward quickly.

There are two keys to the lob. First, as in the cut shot, you need a reasonably good lie so that you can get your club under the ball. Secondly, your swing must be ridiculously slow. The wisest words in golf came, appropriately, from Bobby Jones: "Nobody ever swung a golf club too slowly." On the lob shot, you must try to make Jones a liar.

Take a square stance, with your hands even with the ball, which is played off your left heel. Your wedge or sand wedge should be squared to the pin. Use your own standard grip, and keep your wrists stiff. Your object is to make the laziest Julius Boros swing possible. Just take the club back superslowly and let it drop down on the ball. (Since the sand wedge is heavier than the pitching wedge, it is ideally suited for this shot, assuming you have room to slide its large flange under the ball.)

"Dead-hand" the shot, keeping your wrists stiff throughout the backswing and downswing. This will keep the clubface fully lofted as the blade slips under the ball. The result on a shot of, say, 50 feet should be a high, soft floater that lands, bounces once or twice, and rolls 10 to 30 feet, depending upon the slope and speed of the green.

The lob, like the cut shot, is useful at distances up to 100 yards. However, both shots are most effective at short range—50 yards or less. Like the cut, the lob is also a shot requiring the feel and finesse which come only through practice.

The Pitch-and-Run

The most common variation of the basic pitch is the low, rolling pitch-and-run shot. Essentially a long chip shot, the pitch-and-run is a handy shot for flat, windy courses and big greens.

The shot may be hit with any club from a 3- or 4-iron to a pitching wedge, and many golf teachers insist that several sticks should be considered each time you want to pitch so that you can adapt ideally to your lie, your distance to the green, the distance to the pin from the edge of the green, the slope and grain, and the speed and direction of the wind.

This multi-club philosophy reflects good solid thinking, but it is not necessarily the route most amateurs should follow. Weekend golfers rarely take the time to practice with one club, let alone several clubs for several situations.

A far more sound approach is to hit 90 percent of your pitch-and-runs with the same club, an 8-iron being a good choice. By simply positioning the ball forward or back in your stance you can turn the 8 into a highish-hanging, short roller or a low, long-rolling shot. By practicing with one club the feel and versatility will come quickly.

The basic pitch-and-run is a shot of 20-40 yards that travels about halfway in the air and halfway along the ground. It is hit from a slightly open stance with the feet no more than 10 or 12 inches apart and the clubhead absolutely square to the ball, which should be about midway in the stance. Your hands should be in front of the ball, and most of your weight should be left, to facilitate hitting the ball first and then the grass.

Use a conventional grip, but choke up about two inches, and be sure the back of your left hand is square to your target before you take the club back.

The backswing is all hands and arms, with very little wrist movement. Don't raise the club any higher than just above your belt. As you come back into the ball, be especially firm in the left wrist. Keep that left backhand square to the target and your shot will be just fine.

By positioning the ball an inch or so back in your stance and using the same swing, you'll take several inches of loft off the pitch and add several feet onto the run. Conversely, by moving the ball up toward your left foot you'll produce a higher shot—almost as high as a pitch—that will stop after a couple of bounces and a short run. Practice this shot from a variety of ball positions and you'll develop versatility and confidence with it.

Before you decide to play the pitch-and-run, be sure the terrain permits such a shot. In a classic shot, you want to land the ball about 40 feet short of the stick and let it bounce and roll up stiff. The ideal setting for this shot would be a flat, open green with the pin well back from the front fringe. If the intervening terrain is bumpy, if any hazards guard the green, or if the pin is cut up close to the front of the green, the pitch-and-run is a low-percentage shot. A higher pitch is a better bet, even if you have to hit it into a stiff wind.

Assuming you choose to play a pitch-and-run, always play it in your mind first. Decide exactly where you want the ball to land and how much you want it to roll and break. Visualize the flight of the hypothetical perfect shot, from clubhead to cup. Then take your practice cuts, trying to swing with just enough force to propel the ball to your landing spot.

You can see that as the shots become shorter, the physical demands (at least in terms of power) diminish and the mental game grows in importance.

With the chip shots, this tendency reaches its purest expression. Power becomes irrelevant and accuracy—through thoughtful shot-planning—becomes vital. You may aim a drive at a fairway or an approach shot at a green, but when you address a chip shot your focus suddenly sharpens. Your target is the hole.

As with the pitch-and-run shot, there are two schools of thought regarding proper club selection for chip shots. We have the multi-club school and the single-club school, and once again the one-club philosophy stands out as the wiser course by far.

One club is easier to practice with and is thus easier to master. The pros who advise a multi-club short game all have the time and ability to learn the subtleties of the 4-, 5-, 6-, 7-, 8-, 9-iron and both wedges. For most amateurs such an attempt to maneuver several different lengths, weights, and faces is ridiculous. It's much more intelligent to get to know one club very well.

The club to coddle and cultivate is the pitching wedge. Many golfers, pros and amateurs alike, will argue with this. Some will advocate using the sand wedge or the 8-iron. But the sand wedge is too heavy-headed to swing with rhythm and effectiveness, except when you must do so, in the traps. The mid and short irons (and all those "chipper" clubs sold today) might have been the utility clubs of yesterday when the crude, flat, windy British courses required a skittering short game. But today's rolling, well-watered greens demand shots that can rise and stop as well as spurt and roll. The only club capable of producing both kinds of shots with ease is the pitching wedge.

You could never really *get to know* your 7-iron; it's just too lanky, too concave, too unwieldy. But the pitching wedge, that's a different story. The pitching wedge is the shortest of the green irons, and this comparatively small distance between the clubhead and your hands facilitates "feel," that intangible quality that can either make you or break you as a chipper.

With practice you can develop an affinity with your pitching wedge, an affinity that even your putter will envy! So next time you're around the practice green, make friends with the pitching wedge. It can be the beginning of a long and beautiful relationship.

The Basic Chip

The simplest chip is a 30-footer hit from the short fringe of a level green. All other chips are variations of this basic shot. Here's how to hit it.

Shorten your grip about two inches. This will give you improved control of the club. Take an open stance with your left foot three or four inches back of your target line, and the ball opposite your left heel. Your stance should be so narrow that your heels are no more than 4 or 5 inches apart, and you should be close to the ball—close enough so that your nose is almost over it. Stand straight enough so that your arms are fully extended. About 70 percent of your weight should be left.

The backswing for a chip is about the length of a takeaway

The Basic Chip: Use a pitching wedge, an open stance, and a rearward ball position. Keep your hands close to your body and employ only a pinch of wrist action. Try to feel that your left hand is hitting the ball, and let your follow-through equal your backswing in length.

for any other shot, with the club drawing back about two feet. Your wrists should remain relatively firm with just the slightest cocking motion and your hands should be in front of the club-head. Try to feel your left hand hit the ball. (One good way to develop this feeling is to practice hitting chips with only your left hand, keeping the back of it square to the hole.) The left hand will control the direction of your chip, while the right hand will give it power.

There is virtually no body or leg movement in chipping,

where the stroke is similar to putting: a unified movement of the hands, arms, and wrists. Most important of all, as usual, is to keep your head still and let the club pass cleanly through the ball. Scuffs and bladed shots are often attributable to one thing: an overactive head.

With a 30-foot chip hit from the fringe of the green, you'd normally go for one-third to one-half of the shot in the air and two-thirds to one-half on the ground, depending upon the grain and speed of the green. (If the grain grows against you, expect less roll; if it's with you, count on the ball to run. Naturally, you should play for more roll on fast greens than on slow ones.)

On chips hit from several feet off the green, always try to make the ball land on the green, where its first bounce should be fairly true. If it comes down on the fairway or fringe, anything might happen. When you have no alternative but to make the ball take bounce number one short of the green, bear in mind that hard ground will often cause the ball to take a bound forward, while fringe and soft greenside areas will take something off the ball and cause it to pull up short. If you're unsure of the texture of your hitting area, take a quick walk up and check it out. This little reconnaissance can make the difference between a par and a bogey.

On all chips you should maintain a positive, aggressive attitude. They are not terribly hard or treacherous shots, and consequently should not be played cautiously. When you step up to a common chip of 30 feet or less, don't simply try to get it close— try to sink it.

Of course, most chips are not hit from an ideal lie at a conveniently located pin. That's why you should know how to hit your pitching wedge several different ways.

There are two ways to vary the loft and roll of your chip shots with the pitching wedge. The first of these is to play the ball in different places in your stance. By moving the ball back toward your right heel and letting your hands lead the clubhead you'll decrease the effective loft of the club and promote a low runner. By playing the ball off your left toe and keeping your hands in behind the shot, you'll assure yourself of catching the ball on the upswing with an extra-lofted club, and hitting a chip that accelerates quickly and stays airborne for most of its journey.

The other way to influence the behavior of your chips is to hook or slice them. You don't actually make them bend left or right, but you employ the same principles you use for the intentional type of shots.

By rotating your hands counterclockwise a quarter-turn you will create the weakened slice grip. This, combined with a slightly outward takeaway, will produce a shot with backspin and slice spin, a shot which will fly a bit higher and stop more quickly than the normal square-to-square chip. If you also position the ball forward you'll get even more height from this mini-cut shot, often called a "flip wedge"—an excellent maneuver for fast greens.

Taking a hook grip—rolling your hands a quarter-turn to the right—and making a slightly inside takeaway will effect a low, fast-running shot. You can accentuate this even more by playing the ball back in your stance. This intentionally low chip can be very helpful when you have to climb a bank to the pin.

You can also combine two opposite methods to produce a hybrid shot when the situation calls for one. For instance, you need a fairly high shot to get over a trap, but you also need lots of roll. Play the ball forward in your stance but give it the strong grip and the inside takeaway. Or perhaps you have to chip under a tree limb but make the ball stop quickly on the green. Play the ball back, but use the weak grip and the outside takeaway. Your ball will spurt off the club but check abruptly and roll minimally.

Here is a quick-reference list of the chip shots and how to hit them.

Shot Needed	Ball Position	Grip/Swing Characteristics
Very high with stop	Forward	Slice
High with stop	Forward	Normal
Low with run	Back	Normal
Very low with run	Back	Hook
High with run	Forward	Hook
Low with stop	Back	Slice

Practice these subtle variations, and you'll develop the core of your short-game repertoire.

The Pop Chip
Occasionally you'll get a high lie in the rough or fringe around a green, with the ball sitting up, almost perched, upon the blades

of grass. With such lies it's often better to "pop" the ball out rather than hit down on it as in a conventional chip.

To hit the pop chip, make just one variation in your chipping technique: Keep your wrists absolutely rigid throughout the swing. The best way to ensure a stiff-wristed swing is to point your elbows out to the sides in the old putting stance first popularized by professional Leo Diegel and now practiced by the LPGA's Laura Baugh, among others. Then, just swing back straight and come through the ball in a sweeping pendulum motion. If you position the ball off your left heel, it will pop up smartly and will roll for several feet after hitting the green.

The Run-Up

Now for the 10 percent of your chip shots which should *not* be hit with a pitching wedge.

One of the cardinal rules of chipping, as mentioned earlier, is to land the ball on the green where you can predict with relative accuracy the direction and degree of bounce. Unfortunately an on-green landing is often an impossible luxury. Your lie may be too bare to permit a lofted chip; an overhanging tree limb may prohibit anything but a worm-burner, or the pin may be cut tight at the green's fringe. In these cases you should abandon the conventional chip shot and hit the "run-up" instead.

Rather than lofting half its way and taking one bounce, the run-up takes several small bounces, enabling it to cover ground quickly and climb hills without being deterred.

Choose one of the low-middle irons—the 3, 4, or 5. It doesn't really matter which one, so go with the club that gives you the most confidence. Since you want touch and accuracy, not distance, grip two or three inches down on the club.

Take the half-open stance and play the ball just to the right of your left heel. Use the chip-length backswing, keeping your wrists firm, and lead the club back into the ball, following through toward the hole. This will produce a shot with about a foot of trajectory and a mile of roll.

The Bank Shot

Situation: You're 20 feet from a green which is built on a steep six-foot-high bank. The pin is cut very tight to the bank, and just past the pin the green slopes downhill quickly. There's no percentage in the cut shot, and a run-up is out of the question because the grass on the bank is too shaggy. Solution: the bank shot.

The Bank Shot: Grip down on a 5-iron and punch it firmly into the bank. If you hit the shot right the ball will pop up after hitting the bank, and will drop softly onto the edge of the green. Before hitting the shot be sure to pick both your landing spot on the green and your target on the bank.

The idea with this shot is to smack the ball sharply into the side of the bank. This will cause it to pop up lazily and settle down with a minimum of roll.

Admittedly, the bank shot (sometimes called the "bump" shot) has its risks. If you hit it too high you'll sail clear over the crest. If you hit it too easily you'll get caught in the bank. If you don't hit it into the right area of the bank you'll pop up too little or too much. Nonetheless, when you're in a situation similar to the one just described, the bank shot is the best way out.

First, a couple of "don'ts." Don't hit a bank shot into a straight-upright bank because your ball will not bounce up—only back. The bank must have a forward slope so that the impacting ball will pick up topspin and rise up and over. Don't hit into craggy, thick, or wet banks unless you have no alternative. As with all chip shots, it's best to land the ball on firm, unmarked ground.

Once you determine that your situation favors a bank shot, think things out carefully. This shot poses a unique problem in that you must "land" the ball twice—once on the bank and once on the green or fringe. Decide, first of all, where you want the ball to make its *second* hit, keeping in mind that after this hit its topspin will continue to carry it for several feet, especially if the green slopes away.

Having picked landing spot No. 2, try to guess where on the

bank you will have to punch the ball in order to make it pop up and land on your spot. Be mindful that if you hit high on the bank you'll have to hit harder because you'll get less jump than if you hit near the base. A low shot may even climb up the bank. Generally, however, it's better to go with this firm hit to the top of the bank and play for a quiet bounce.

The appropriate weapon here is a choked-down 5-iron, though if you're close to the bank (10 feet or less) you may want to hit a 6- or 7-iron.

The shot you want to hit is sort of a punched chip. Play the ball back in the middle of your slightly open stance and keep your hands well forward. Take a short, stiff-wristed backswing and sock the back of the ball. Close your eyes and cross your fingers!

The bank shot and run-up are especially useful on two-level greens. When the pin is on the elevated back half of a two-level green, but just at the brink of the hill, you may have to try a soft bank shot with your pitching wedge. If, on the other hand, the pin is well back on the upper level, a run-up will climb the hill nicely.

Play the Break

Of course, chip shots can bounce and roll sideways as well as up and down. When you face a chip to a sidehill green it's important to read the break just as you would on a putt.

Too many golfers fail to read greens when chipping. Instead of aiming 10 feet to the side of the cup and letting the ball roll stiff they invariably hit *at* the cup and watch the shot drift 10 feet to the right or left.

There are a couple of thoughts to keep in mind when playing the break for a chip or pitch shot. First, be aware that the harder you hit the ball, the less it will break, just as strong putts break less than lags. Break is dependent upon trajectory, too. In general, pitch shots break less than chips. The high flyers, with little rolling distance, will naturally be influenced to a lesser degree than the low runners, which hit early and cover most of their yardage on the putting surface. On a bi-level green you may conceivably face a shot that forces you to play 20 feet of right-hand break if putting, and no break—or even a few feet of *left*-hand break—if you chip. It all depends upon where you land the ball.

If you hit a mini-slice or cut chip, be ready for the ball to

The Uphill Chip: Play the ball in the middle of your open stance, and keep 80 percent of your weight on your left side. Take the club back down the slope and lead it back up and into the ball, with a little more force than you'd use for a level chip of the same distance.

move an inch or so to the right on a level green. If the green also leans down to the right, then play lots of break on a cut chip, because the slope will multiply the slice spin you impart to such a chip, and the ball will dive right when it hits the green. Conversely, a cut-chip hit into a hill that slopes from right to left will tend to work against the slope and will not break as markedly as a squarely hit chip will. Knowing this can make the difference between a knee-knocker and a gimme for your par.

These are the nuances of chipping. Give them thought and practice, and they'll eventually come to you naturally. In effect, you'll develop a sixth sense around the green. You won't have to think through situations, just compute them subconsciously and apply your knowledge of speed, spin, distance, and break.

If you think there are subtleties involved in chipping *to* hills, consider the complexities in chipping to hills *from* hills. Ever since the braes of St. Andrews golfers have had to contend with uneven footing around the green. And if you don't know how to scramble from these situations, then you don't know how to scramble.

Uphill

Because so many greens are elevated or banked, the most common of the hilly greenside lies is the uphill lie. And the most common mistake on this most common lie is to leave the ball uncommonly short of the cup. What most golfers fail to recognize is that an uphill lie adds loft and subtracts distance. So when

The Downhill Chip: Take a wide-open stance, with the ball positioned just off your right toe. The right knee should be flexed and the clubface should be open. Lead into impact with your hands, and hit firmly down and across the ball.

you hit the ball with what you deem to be sufficient power, some of the horizonal distance is converted into vertical distance, elevation. The ball pops up, plops down, and stops short.

Two obvious corrective methods: One, use an 8-iron instead of a wedge. Hit the same shot and let the club do the work for you. Two, play the wedge but move it back to the middle of your stance, so that 80 percent of your weight is uphill. Take the club back down the slope and hit back up along the slope and into the ball. This together with just a bit more "oomph" should get you the extra distance you need.

Downhill

With a downhill chip, the central problem is still one of loft, but in this case it is an insufficiency of loft that plagues nine shots out of ten. When leaning downhill we all have difficulty getting the club under the ball for a clean, crisp shot. The result—even when the shot is hit with a wedge—is a low, skittering shot. This is fine when you have plenty of green to work with, but when the pin is in a tight spot, so are you.

Increasing the loft on a downhill chip is not quite as simple as decreasing it for an uphill chip, but there are a couple of things you can do.

First, you can use a more lofted club—the only one in your bag—the sand wedge. Just be sure your lie is fluffy enough for you to slide that fat flange under the ball. If it isn't you'll just compound your problem, and probably skull the shot.

The surest way to even out a downhill chip is to stay with

the pitching wedge and make a couple of height-conducive adjustments. Take a well-opened stance with the ball positioned just off your right toe, and with most of your weight downhill. The right knee should be flexed slightly more than usual. This will level out your stance and help you get down and under the ball. Make a cut-swing takeaway, bring the club back on a markedly outside path. Lead the club out and up the slope with a quick wrist break. Bring it back along the same path—down and across the bank and into the ball. Concentrate on contacting the ball before the hill. And, please, stay down, if you want the ball to get up. Don't quit on this shot, be firm, because if you hit it properly it will not jump at all, it will sit quickly.

Sidehill Lies
The two other lies you run into around the green—and everywhere else—are the sidehill lies, one with the ball above your feet and the other with the ball below.

When the ball is on a higher level than your feet, make two simple adjustments. Shorten your grip an inch or two, to avoid stubbing the club on the ground. And allow for a natural pull to the left by aiming right an appropriate number of inches or feet, depending on the slope of the green.

For the sidehill lie with the ball below your feet, beware of the shank. To avoid it, concentrate on keeping your weight back on your heels. This will help prevent you from leaning or tipping forward and "hoseling" the ball. A more upright stance and a full-length grip will also aid the cause. Since you'll have a tendency to push a shot from this lie, close the clubface just a pinch, and aim a bit left of where you would from a level lie.

From the Rough
If you're in deep, thick grass beside the green you often have a real problem. You need a true finesse shot, a shot that is strong enough to get out of the rough but not so strong that it jumps out and sails over the green.

The best maneuver is to take your sand wedge and play an explosion similar to the blast from sand. This will produce a soft shot that will get you out of trouble without putting you back in. Address the shot with an open, narrow stance and the ball off your right heel. Your hands should be well forward, and you should be gripping the club more tightly than usual, especially with your left hand. Keep your clubface open.

With your eyes fixed on a spot two inches in back of the ball, take a long, lazy, upright backswing and come down firmly on your aim spot. Swing through fully (as a general rule, hit the ball about twice as hard as you would a chip from the fringe). Don't let the blade close through impact. The ball should float up and onto the green, just like a sand explosion. Also like the explosion, the ball will lack backspin, so expect a fair amount of roll and play to land the ball early.

This same basic shot should be used to hit short shots from sandy rough, pine needles, and leaves, although each of these has its own idiosyncrasies. Generally, you won't have to swing as hard from these surfaces as you would from thick grass.

Hardpan

Bare ground around the green can be troublesome, but fortunately there are several ways to handle it. In many cases the best way to deal with these hardpan lies is to hit the same explosion shot mentioned above. Just blast into the ground about two inches behind the ball. If you're also standing on hardpan, be careful not to pivot or shift your weight too much. When hit correctly, the explosion from bare ground has plenty of backspin and stops quickly or even backs up after hitting the green.

If you're in a situation where you don't need a lot of height on the shot, you can pinch-punch the ball from hardpan, causing a low-flying pitch-and-run that skips and settles after a few feet of roll.

Play the ball in the middle of your slightly open stance. Hit it with a square clubface and a punch swing, leading the club through with your hands. The wrists should be stiff, the backswing low and slow, and the follow-through short and low. Be sure to pinch the ball, to hit both it and the hardpan at precisely the same time. Swing slowly and steadily and you'll have no trouble.

Of course, if you're on hardpan and you need no loft at all, then by all means use your putter. Why go to the trouble of blasting or pinching when you can roll the ball onto the green?

The Texas Wedge

The Texas wedge is a good club to hit whenever it's a viable possibility for the simple reason that most of us are better putters than chippers. The whole trick is in deciding intelligently when and when not to putt from off the green. As just men-

The Texas Wedge: Try to judge the rolling speeds of both the fringe and the green. Then just hit a good, confident putt.

tioned, hardpan is a good place, assuming your surface is firm and even all the way to the green. In such a situation you should be able to read the speed and break of your putt with confidence. If you can't, it's probably better to chip.

When reading putts from off the green, keep in mind that the ball will often have two rolling speeds—one from your position to the edge of the green, and then a faster speed on the putting surface. You should do your best to assess this effect and hit the ball with an amount of force that will allow it to switch gears at the fringe of the green.

One of the skills of scrambling is being able to make two or three different clubs hit the same shot. That way, no club in your bag will be indispensable, *not even the putter.*

The Rhode Island Putter: Using your normal putter grip, stance and swing, pop the center of the ball with the leading edge of your sand wedge.

The Rhode Island Putter

Did you know you can putt effectively with your sand wedge? Well, you can, and while it's not recommended for most three-footers, this shot can be useful from just off the green. Often a chip shot from thick fringe can be difficult and risky. The grass has a tendency to catch your pitching wedge and turn it or divert it off line, causing a less-than-accurate shot.

Take your normal putting grip, play the ball up off your left foot, and just bump the center of the ball with the leading edge of the wedge. The big flange of the sand wedge will glide smoothly through the heavy fringe and will produce a shot that hops out of the fringe and then rolls to the pin.

Don't try this one without practice. It requires a precise pop to the back of the ball, and not everyone can pull it off on command—not even Jack Nicklaus, who tried this shot on the 71st hole of the 1975 U.S. Open at the Medinah Country Club and hit it 20 feet past the hole. So practice hitting this shot before you make a practice of hitting it!

A good short game is your best friend. It turns bogeys into pars and pars into birdies. It gives you confidence on your full shots and allows you tremendous latitude in planning your tee-to-green strategy. Finally, it's a great asset in match play. There's nothing like a few one-putt greens for raising your spirits and lowering those of your opponent.

sand play

"The sand shot ought to be the easiest shot in golf," Walter Hagen once said. "You don't even have to hit the ball." Of course, it was simple for Hagen to scratch his head and chuckle at the irony. He won five PGA's, four British Opens, two U.S. Opens, and dozens of lesser titles because, in part, he knew what he was doing when he swaggered into a trap.

For most of us it's another story. On the casual golfer's list of favorite places, sand traps rank somewhere between shark tanks and leper colonies. He approaches them with trepidation and leaves them—often much later—in defeat.

It all boils down to the same old chain—fear due to lack of confidence, lack of confidence due to previous failure to perform, failure to perform due to lack of practice on the basics.

Golfers think they can "pick up" an ability to hit sand shots just by playing them as they come. Unfortunately the sand game does not come through osmosis. You must first learn a few fundamentals, and learn them well. Building on this base, you can go ahead and pick up the fine points with experience.

The Explosion: Use a wristy, three-quarter backswing, with a minimum of pivot and leg movement. On the way down, pull through the shot with your left hand, and penetrate the sand about two inches behind the ball. Delay your wrist release until after impact.

First of all, if you don't have a sand wedge, get one. Like the pitching wedge, it is invaluable. Ever since 1932, when Gene Sarazen created this strange club with the wide-open face and heavy flange and used it to win both the British Open and U.S. Open, the sand wedge has been virtually the only club to hit from a trap.

Ninety percent of all sand shots are variations on two techniques—the explosion and the splash. If you can hit these shots effectively—well enough to get up and down, say, one out of three times—then your sand game is pretty sound.

The Explosion

The standard explosion shot is used to raise a ball from a moderately good lie—not buried, but not ideal, either. To hit it, take an open stance, with your hips and shoulders aimed two to three feet left of your landing point. Be sure your footing and balance are secure by really digging in with your spikes. This will also give you a good clue to the texture of the sand. Shorten up on the grip to compensate for the fact that, by digging into the sand, you have decreased the distance between your hands and the ball. Assuming you have a level lie, the ball should be played off your left instep. Your clubface should be square to the target, and 70 percent of your weight should be on your left side.

Break your wrists quickly on the backswing, but do everything else slowly and smoothly, with a three-quarter swing, a minimum of pivot and weight shift, and almost no leg and body movement. On the downswing, the hands should be out front, promoting a downward blow. Concentrate on making your club enter the sand about two inches behind the ball, and keep your eye on that point of entry, not on the ball itself.

The exact distance to hit behind the ball will vary, as you'll see, according to the nature of the lie, the type and texture of the sand, and the distance your shot must cover. However, the old "dollar bill" rule—where you imagine the ball to be sitting on George Washington's face and you try to cut into the sand at a point where the bill's edge would be—is still a good guide. Since you never get much backspin on a full explosion, allow for plenty of roll.

The Splash

The splash is the other staple of sand play. In truth, the splash is itself a variation of the explosion, a sort of skim-explosion with

The Splash: Since you want to take a shallower "divot" of sand than in the explosion, play the ball up off your left heel. Make a lower, wider take-away than you would for the explosion, and try to skim about two inches behind and an inch under the ball with an open clubface. The result will be a far less sandy shot, and more backspin on the ball when it hits the green.

lots of backspin. It may be used for great accuracy from good and moderately good lies.

As with the explosion, dig in deep for good balance. Take a wide open stance, with the ball off your left instep, your hands behind the ball, and most of your weight left. With this shot, however, you should hold the club so that the face is a bit open and the back of the club is nearly flat against the sand. This clubhead angle will encourage the club to bounce off the sand rather than dig into it, as in the explosion.

Make a low, slow takeaway—don't lift up as abruptly as you would for the explosion—and bring your hands only to about shoulder height. Keep your eye on an area about two inches behind the ball, and, as you swing down, concentrate on entering the sand *shallowly* at that spot and skimming under the ball. Keep a steady head to ensure that you make a precise, shallow cut.

An important feature of all sand play, and a part often neglected, is the follow-through. Don't leave the club in the sand or your ball will also stay there. As for the force of the swing, follow this rule of thumb: Hit the shot with about half the power you'd use for a pitch shot of the same distance.

The differences between this splash method and the explosion are as follows: Since your hands are back, you'll be less likely to make the downward blow characteristic of the explosion. This, together with the wide-open clubface, will give you a high shot that pops up on a thin layer of sand and sits down nicely, or even spins back, when it hits the green. This makes it a more aggressive shot than the explosion. Practice will show you that you play for very little roll on the splash shot.

The explosion and the splash are the two basics you should know, but by themselves, they aren't enough. In the course of an 18-hole round, it's not uncommon to have a half-dozen lies in the sand, each posing a different problem, each demanding a different shot. If you hit the classic explosion or splash from these lies, you'll probably get them all out, but you won't get them all close.

In order to be consistently accurate from sand, you have to be able to adapt the two main shots to the idiosyncrasies of the various situations—to the depth of your lie, the consistency of the sand, the steepness of the trap's bank, and the distance to the pin. Let's look at some of these problems and match them with appropriately doctored explosions and splashes.

From footprints and fried eggs, use the explosion shot, penetrating the sand at the edge of the footprint and the yolk of the egg. As with all explosions, expect plenty of roll.

From a perched lie in the sand, chip the ball whenever possible. When you can't chip, lay the clubface back, and open it up. Then try your best to cut cleanly under the ball. Don't forget to follow through on this shot.

The Buried (Plugged) Ball

Most of us play this shot with too much muscle and too little finesse. The shot to hit is the explosion, but with one variation—a square, slightly hooded clubface. By hooding the face you'll allow the club to dig deeper into the sand and pry the ball out of its grave.

Just move your hands forward a bit at address and/or reposition the ball in your open stance so that it is in a rearward position. You will get no backspin from this shot, so pick a spot well short of the pin, allow for plenty of break, and swing easy. Concentrate on precision rather than power.

Ball *Really* Buried

For those lies where only the top of the ball is visible, use the same explosion shot just described, but just this once, trade in the sand wedge for the pitching wedge. The thinner flange will facilitate the extra-deep penetration needed to raise the ball. Use a quick wrist-break and a descending hit which allows you to dig as deeply as possible while still permitting a follow-through.

Footprints and Fried Eggs

For both of these situations you should use the explosion shot with the club closed for "digability." Dig down under the ball, starting at the white of the egg or the edge of the footprint (regardless of the size of the blowout). Also, exaggerate the firm downward blow. As always with the explosion, play for several feet of roll.

The Perched Lie

While just the opposite of the plugged ball, the perched ball is no less troublesome to amateur golfers.

If at all possible you should chip this shot out, according to the method described in the previous chapter. But if you have a lip in your way, or you must stop the ball, then a soft, careful splash is what you want. Actually you want to make direct contact with the ball, with little or no sand-divot at all. If you take too much sand on this shot, you may whiff under it, because a perched lie usually does not offer enough of a cushion of sand to carry the ball out of the trap.

Open the face of the club wide, and lay it back too. Then "walk around" the open, laid-back clubhead until you reach a comfortable open stance. Swing softly but comfortably, and do your best to cut just under the ball. If you hit this shot properly, you'll get a lot of backspin, so don't play for too much roll.

Uphill Lies

Since most traps are bowls (or at least plates) you will have plenty of hilly lies in the sand.

With an uphill lie in a trap the secret is much the same as it is for the uphill fairway lie described in Chapter 3, and for the uphill chip in Chapter 6. The whole idea is to balance your body so that your hips, shoulders, and knees are parallel to the up-sloping bank of the trap. Lean back just a bit, flex your left knee,

From an uphill lie, hit a soft explosion but penetrate the sand just an inch behind the ball instead of two inches. Use a little extra force as well.

From a downhill lie, explode the ball but hit the sand three or four inches behind the ball, and really hit down on it. Expect more roll than with any other sand shot.

and experiment until you have a semblance of equilibrium and a solid footing in the sand.

Hit a soft explosion shot, with one small but important variation: Penetrate the sand a bit closer to the ball, about an inch to an inch and a half back for a moderate lie. With an uphill lie the sand gets deeper after your club enters it. You'll be digging up a big, deep cushion naturally, so you don't need to take much sand behind the ball.

Expect the higher-than-normal shot that all uphill lies produce, and compensate by cutting into the sand with a little extra force and making a conscious effort to follow through. The high shot will also stop more quickly than most blasts, so play for a bit less roll than you would from a level lie.

Downhill Lie

This is probably the toughest of all trap shots, especially if your ball is sitting poorly or you're hitting to a green that slopes away.

Once again, the first thing to do is level up the plane of your swing. Adjust your footing and address position until your belt is parallel to the downsloping bank. Play the ball back in your open stance. This will help promote the sharply up-and-down swing this shot demands. Also, open the face of your club and lay it back so that it lies almost flat on the sand. The wide-open face is necessary because your downhill stance reduces the natural loft of the club.

Remember the principle of the sand shot—riding the ball out on a cushion of sand and don't try to "lift" the ball out. You must hit down and into the sand—three or four inches behind the ball, in this case, because the depth of the sand is shallower in front of the ball than in back. Lead down and under with the hands, and follow through. Just after impact, both the ball and your hands should be moving at the green, but at nearly perpendicular angles.

Since you almost never get backspin from a downhill trap lie, play for lots and lots of roll. If the pin is tight or the green slopes away you'll just have to try to hit as high and lazy a shot as you can, and then hope for the best.

Sidehill Lie—Ball Above Feet

Here, again, you'll find similarities to the fairway and chip shots from this lie. As with all hilly lies, the first thing to do is to align yourself. In this case, simply point yourself a few feet to the right of your intended landing spot.

Shorten your grip a bit to make up for the heightened ball position. Then, if you aren't buried, hit a smooth splash shot, being sure to keep your left wrist firm. This hook-promoting lie has a tendency to force a flat swing, with an accompanying roll of the wrists. So remember, it's important to keep your left wrist square to the hole throughout the swing, and concentrate on doing just that.

Sidehill Lie—Ball Below Feet

As usual, the tactics are just opposite to those for sidehill lie No. 1. Expect the shot to go right, and compensate by aiming a few feet left of your objective. With this lie there's a reasonable danger of hitting a shank, so be sure to dig in well and hit down on the ball. Swing slowly and smoothly, and keep your head rock-still.

When You Need Lots of Distance

The sand shot of 50 to 100 yards is regarded almost universally as the hardest shot in golf. It can be hit with either an explosion or splash swing, depending upon your lie.

If the lie is good—the ball is sitting up or is only slightly depressed in the sand—use the splash shot. Take a smooth, full (meaning three-quarter) swing and bring the club back on an

outside path. Come back down and across the ball, penetrating the sand shallowly about two inches in back of the ball, and skim it out smartly.

This long cut shot will rise quickly and stop just as quickly when it hits the green, so go right for the pin. The shot is useful right up to the full length of your sand wedge, and thereafter you can use the pitching wedge for similar effect.

When you're half-buried or in worse shape, try the long explosion. Square the face of your sand wedge, close up your open stance a bit, and take a fuller swing than you would for most trap shots, hitting firmly down and through the ball. The important adjustment here is to take less sand than you would for a greenside explosion. Remember all those booboos that sailed way over the green? They were caused by the fact that you took too little sand. For the long explosion, however, you *want* to take less sand than usual. So remember those bad shots, and try to hit one on purpose. The less sand you take, the farther your ball will go.

When You Need Lots of Height

We've all been in those traps that are so deep you feel as if you're hitting out of the Grand Canyon. In these situations your mission, should you decide to accept it, is to hit a high, high shot, a shot that can travel two to three times farther in the air than it does horizontally.

Since even the standard sand shot demands a fast-rising trajectory, the supersteep shot requires exaggeration of all the sand-play techniques.

Let's assume you have to raise the ball 10 feet to get it up onto the green. First of all, if you're buried or even half-buried, forget about pulling off any miracles. The same is true if your lie is downhill or in a footprint or fried egg. Don't try the finesse shot; play to the safe side, even if it means hitting directly away from the pin. There are some shots in golf that mere mortals are incapable of hitting, and the high, steep explosion from a bad lie is one of them.

You have to play a cut-splash, which means you must have a

The Long Explosion Shot: Use a wide takeaway, a full backswing, and plenty of leg movement on your way into the ball. At impact try to duplicate all those overly thin shots you've rocketed across greens. Remember that the less sand you take, the farther the ball will go.

relatively clean, uncovered, unsunken lie. If you do, then begin by taking an extremely open stance, with your left foot pulled back five to six inches from a square-stance alignment. Open your sand wedge wide, too, and lay it on its back, playing the ball off your left toe.

Your takeaway should be just like that for a cut shot—sharply upward and outward. On the downswing, come back down and across, and try to slip that open wedge just under the ball, taking as little sand as possible. Follow through forcefully, or you may not get all ten of those vertical feet.

The cut splash is much tougher than the cut shot, since the ball sits flat on the sand rather than being supported by a couple of dozen blades of grass. As you can imagine, it's vital to have a smooth, quiet swing and a rock-steady head. Without these two virtues, you'll never make the precise hit that is crucial to the success of this shot.

Different Consistencies of Sand

When the sand is of a light, powdery consistency, expect less resistance to the club, and thus, better digging power. As a consequence you'll have to hit about a half-inch farther behind the ball in order to compress the grains enough to give the ball a ride out. Expect more backspin on your splash shots and less roll from your explosions when your milieu is powdery sand.

Coarse, tightly packed sand has just the opposite effect. It's tougher to penetrate and it requires that you hit relatively close to the ball. The coarse sand prevents the club from getting a good bite on the ball, so your shots will all roll more than from normal or powdery sand.

In wet weather the sand will be tightly packed and your sand wedge won't be able to dig as deeply as it does in dry sand. This heavy-flanged club will have a tendency to bounce off the sand and cause a skulled shot. The same bounce effect occurs in shots from shallow sand. In such cases you're well advised to hit your shots with the sharper-flanged pitching wedge. For a covered lie, open the blade slightly and use the normal explosion technique. However, swing a bit more easily. Hit about two inches behind the ball and keep your follow-through low and short. If you have a good lie, go ahead with a standard splash shot, hit with a pitching wedge and a gentler-than-usual touch. If the trap's lip is low, you should consider chipping the ball out.

When you have a good lie and the trap's lip is negligible, try a chip shot from sand. Play it as you would any other chip, and be sure to hit down and through the ball.

Hard sand, a good lie, and a lipless trap are perfect conditions for a putt.

Chipping from Sand

A chip from sand is an intelligent shot when you have a good lie and the trap's lip is not high. Play it with your pitching wedge and hit it as you would a normal chip: ball back, shortened grip, and firm downward hit. Don't make the common mistake of trying too hard to "pick it clean." Just keep your head very still and chip it off with an arm-and-shoulder swing.

Putting from Sand

Firm, level sand, a good lie, and absence of a lip can be excellent conditions for a putt from a trap. Try to gauge the amount of power you'll need by eyeing your intended path a couple of times. Then line up the ball in the center of your stance and give it a smooth, even stroke.

Although the putt from sand is best when hit from the ideal conditions mentioned above, it's a good shot to keep in mind when the pin position is tight, even if the sand is normal and there's a small lip. You can often play a nice shot by rolling the ball up the bank and letting it ski-jump onto the green. It will usually stop quickly.

By hitting a standard explosion shot with a choked-down 6-iron, you'll produce a medium-trajectory shot that will run like a scared jackrabbit. It's a perfect shot to hit when you have a long way to the pin.

This may look strange but it works. From a buried lie, if you address the ball with a super-hooded clubface you'll explode it from the small pocket of the club where the heel of the wedge meets the hosel. This will result in a much less active ball than with a normal explosion. On occasion you'll actually get backspin from a buried lie.

Trick Shots from Sand
In truth, the last place to get cute is the sand trap. Sand play calls for cautious thinking and adherence to the basics. Only after a great deal of practice will you gain the expertise and confidence to enable you to try the next two shots. But since they both work well, here they are. Good luck.

The 6-Iron Explosion
This is the shot to hit when you want to roll the ball a long, long way. By hitting the standard explosion with a choked-down 6-iron you'll produce a mid-height explosion that will take one bounce and then scoot into a long roll. It's really not a tough shot, but you should approach it with caution for the simple reason that a 6-iron is rarely used for explosion shots—and for good reason.

The Intentional Shank-Explosion

Let's say you have a buried or semi-buried lie and the pin position is tight. With the explosion shot this lie requires, you'll never stop the ball close to the pin, because you can't put any backspin on the ball. Your one solution is the shank-explosion. In this shot you actually try to shank the buried ball. In so doing you'll explode the ball from the small pocket where the heel of the sand wedge meets the hosel. Hitting the ball with this cupped pocket will produce a less active shot that will stop a great deal faster than a normal blast.

As you set up for this shot, rotate the club 90 degrees counterclockwise, address the ball with the pocket of your sand wedge, and *aim at least 10 feet right of where you want to land the ball.* Also, be sure to follow through. This magical shot can save your day—and ruin your opponent's—very quickly.

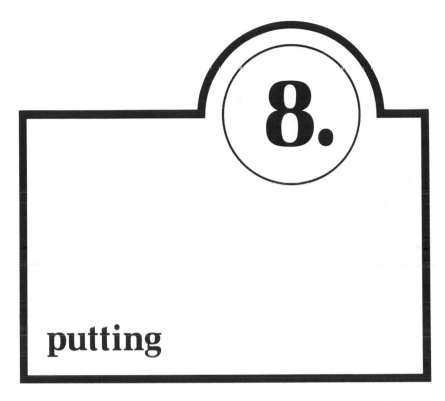

8.

putting

Ben Hogan hated putting, and for good reason. He wasn't very good at it—at least not compared to the rest of his game. No one ever hit a golf ball from tee to green with greater accuracy or consistency than The Hawk did in his prime. On the putting green, however, Ben didn't have the jump on anyone. His lament is understandable:

You work all your life to perfect a repeating swing that will get you to the greens, and then you have to try to do something that is totally unrelated. There shouldn't be any cups, just flagsticks, and the man who hit the most fairways and greens and got closest to the pins would be the tournament winner.

Ironically, most of us can find encouragement in Hogan's misery. For most of us do not have, nor will we ever have, Hogan's native shot-making ability. Yet any of us is capable of becoming a deadly putter.

The putt requires no trajectory and no backspin or sidespin

of any kind. There are rarely any hazards to consider, and your lie is nearly always perfect. All you have to do is roll the ball a few feet into a opening twice its width, an assignment which requires relatively little in terms of coordinated power, at least when you consider the demands of the shots which get you to the green. Indeed, if 50 percent of golf is putting, one may argue that any player age 7 to 97 has at least half a chance to become the best in the world.

Standing over a 40-foot putt, most of us are equals, whether we reached the green in two with a 280-yard drive and a neatly feathered 4-iron, or in seven after a series of 60-yard chops. Anyone can make a 40-footer—and even the best putters will miss it nine times out of ten.

For this reason, the putting green should be the happy haven of all amateur golfers, a place where the sins of the previous 400 yards are redressed, where strokes are made up, never lost.

But this is hardly the case. The average amateur's putting ability is far from awesome. While the pros one-putt nearly a third of the greens they hit, taking about 30 putts per round, amateurs, as a body, average fully *10* more, or about 40 putts for 18 holes. This sad statistic becomes even more shameful when you consider that amateurs often hit to greens with their third, fourth, and fifth shots, meaning they're usually approaching from shorter distances than the pros do and, presumably, they are leaving themselves shorter putts.

The problem is not in technique—at least not in the grip-stance-swing sense, because there *is* no correct method of putting. Look at the pros. Trevino has a wide stance, Palmer is knock-kneed; Weiskopf leans left, Nicklaus dips right. Sure, they all have a few important things in common—a firm stance, a steady head, a smooth takeaway—but ultimately, putting is a Machiavellian exercise: Whatever works is right.

Therefore, no physical "how-to" will be presented here. Like most scrambling shots, putting must be fitted both to your own needs and to the idiosyncrasies of the situation. Indeed, you may change your stance, ball position, and stroke from round to round, hole to hole, or even from one putt to the next, if, on each putt and with each new grip, stance, and stroke you feel comfortable and confident, because comfort and confidence are the beginning of every successful putt.

Attitude and Aptitude

Putting is actually a vicious cycle of attitude and aptitude, confidence and touch. To have one or the other is to have both. No great putter can be accurate without knowing he's accurate, nor can he be self-assured without assuring himself with several dropped putts.

Of the two, attitude is by far the more important. If you can develop a good head, the hands and arms will take care of themselves.

At the center of a sound putting attitude is the aggressiveness mentioned earlier in this book. A ravenous hunger for the cup should control your actions from the minute your approach shot comes to rest.

Why be so vicious about it? Because, unlike the longer shots, every putt is a do-or-die proposition. You can always make up for a bad drive with a good second shot, or make up for a bad second shot with a good chip. But there's no way to scramble out of a bad putt—a putt missed is a stroke lost.

So gear yourself to making every putt you ever address, whether it's 2 feet or 30 yards. Never, never lag the ball. Lagging is associated with a fear of three-putting, and such negative thinking has no business in the scrambler's game, least of all on the putting green. When putting, you should channel your mind and body toward one goal—hitting the ball firmly into the middle of the cup.

You can, and often should, play a cautious iron shot off the tee of a tight hole or aim your approach shot safely for the fat part of a green. But once you're sitting perfectly on the green, you have to go for the hole. You must attack.

Many of the golf's best minds will disagree with this "never-up, never-in" philosophy. Not the least of them is Bobby Jones, a thoughtful and articulate writer on golf as well as the game's most fabled player. On the subject of never-up, never-in putting, Jones wrote: "It is true that I will never know that the putt which did not get to the cup might have gone in. But one thing I am positive about: the putt which rolled past the cup definitely didn't go in."

Very true. And yet, if Bobby had just reached the hole with every putt he ever hit, consider the number of putts Calamity Jane would have drained. Always up, more often in!

Arnold Palmer in his prime embodied putting aggressiveness

142

better than anyone before or since. Even Jack Nicklaus acknowledges the early-'60s Palmer to be "the best putter I have ever seen." In those days Palmer putted accurately, consistently, and *boldly*. The green is where the Palmer "charge" made its name.

Charge Your Putts

Being a bold putter does not mean grossly overshooting the hole with every off-line putt. To be productively aggressive on the green, you need to make just one small alteration in your putting tack. Instead of trying to stop your ball at the lip of the cup, try to hit it with enough force to make it die just a couple of inches past the cup. Most instruction books will tell you to hit the ball just hard enough so that its last revolution will take it into the cup. But it's wiser to give your putt one or two extra revolutions of power—enough to let it *roll into* the cup, not just drop.

This charge method of putting has several advantages. The most obvious of these has been mentioned—you always get the ball to the hole and thus have at least a chance of sinking every putt. However, there are certain less visible but no less important benefits attached to a bold putting stroke.

First, boldness means firmness of stroke, and a firm, smooth stroke is one of the few physical requirements of good putting.

Secondly, firmness of stroke can ride the eternal cycle and return as confidence. If you know you're getting the ball up to the hole you can develop that strange "I'm-going-to-make-this-one" feeling. Chronic shortness, on the other hand, breeds a fear and a lack of faith in the stroke.

Thirdly, by hitting putts boldly, you play for less break, which is a wise thing to do. For one thing, you leave less to chance by taking the straighter route to the hole. You will be less susceptible to the literal rub of the green, the subtle but inevitable bumps, bellies, and bits of drek that lie in every putt's path. Let your stroke, not the green, get the ball to the cup. A firmer stroke means a smoother-rolling putt.

Fourthly, hitting bold, straight putts is good training for the two- and three-footers. Very few of the "character-builders" should be looped in. If you simply hit them crisply at the middle of the cup, they'll go in. A consistently firm stroke will help you here. You'll rarely have to "give up the cup."

Fifthly, though they shouldn't even be mentioned, second putts must be considered. And second putts are normally easier if they're coming back over the same area they've just covered. In

Putting is a Machiavellian exercise. Whatever works is right.

general, it's easier to find your way *back* to a place you've just passed than it is to cross untested terrain. The same is true with putting. By getting the ball up to the hole every time, you can observe the speed and break of the grass that surrounds the cup. Normally your return putt will break in exactly the opposite direction of your first putt—and you will have evidence to that effect.

Sixthly, and last, you'll be able to narrow down and identify the reasons you miss your putts, and then correct your mistakes. There are four ways to miss a putt—short, long, left, and right. By reaching the hole every time, you immediately eliminate one of those reasons for error. At the same time you allow yourself to take "data" on your putting habits. Many

golfers tend to mis-aim their putts, and if they leave those putts short, too, it's often hard to detect the error, since the grain and slope near the cup can't be factored in. But if your ball always gets to the cup, you'll be able to see it go too hard or too far left or right. More important, you'll remember that image and, ideally, will take steps to correct it.

Think aggressively, stroke boldly, and you'll have a good start on the "attitude" half of putting. Firmness, however, is nothing without finesse, so let's look at the other half of putting —aptitude.

Touch

Putting aptitude is normally called "touch," and putting touch is probably the most misunderstood concept in golf.

We've all heard the philosophy that touch is like perfect pitch—either you have it or you don't. That's about as true as a cobblestone putting green. There are indeed varying degrees of putting ability, just as there are varying abilities in pitching pennies or bunting a baseball or sinking a foul shot. Each of us is born with a different blend of coordination and cool muscle and nerve. But there is no such thing as a natural touch, and nothing prevents the average golfer from developing a very good touch.

Moreover, the touch that comes through work and experience is a strong, confident, and lasting touch. The guy "born with a hot hand" is apt to lose it as quickly as he discovers it, and when he loses that touch he, too, is lost, unable to rebuild it. But for the guy who develops his touch, a lapse is rarely an unnerving experience. He knows he has established an effective stroke, and that knowledge alone will enable him to weather most cold spells.

The Two Halves of Touch

Another widespread misunderstanding has to do with the actual senses involved in touch. Many instructors will tell you that touch is a feeling in the hands. This is reasonable, since the very word is synonymous with "feel," the sense of touch.

However, touch is more than a pressure sensation of the putter in your hands. It is actually an interaction of feel and sight, taction and perception. That hot hand is useless if it isn't paired with a good eye. If putting were only "feel" then the best putters would be the congenitally blind, who develop an extra-sensitive tactile sense.

At least half of touch is the ability to see the grain and contour of the green and relate the distance and break to your hands. Here, again, good physical ability is not enough. You can have the vision of an astronaut, but unless you focus it on the problems of putting, it will do you no good at all. And like the tactile side of touch, the perceptive side must be developed through practice.

The tactile side of putting is established and refined by grooving your stroke, by hitting putt after putt until you have molded the fundamentals to fit your own needs and comfort. This is something one learns on a practice green, not in this book.

The perceptive ability is another story. It is *not* subject to personal improvisation and accommodation. There are several fundamentals of green reading which should be learned and followed to the letter. Since this visual side of putting is often neglected, it will not be neglected here. View the following few pages as the only hard-and-fast "how-to" rules a scrambling putter needs to know.

Reading the Green

Sinking a sidehill putt involves a whole lot more than just "playing the break." Grain, height, thickness, and texture of the grass all help determine the way the ball will roll. So can the time of day, the speed of the wind, the nature of the surrounding terrain, and even the state and locality you're playing in.

Only experience can tell you how much to allow for each of these factors. It helps, however, to know something about each of them. If you can come to grips with this visual side of putting, the tactile will come much more easily—and much less frequently.

Grain

Except for the actual contour of the green, the force that influences a putt to the greatest degree is the grain of the grass. "Grain" refers to the direction in which the blades of grass are growing—and they're almost always pointing one way or another.

Fortunately, it's easy to determine the direction of a green's grain. As you approach the green, simply observe its "finish." If it seems to have a sheen, the grass is growing in the same direction you're walking and the grain is with you. If, on the other hand, the putting surface looks dull, the grain is against you.

An even better way to be sure of the grain is to scrape the blade of your putter along the fringe of the green. If the putter

One good way to check the direction of the grain is to rub your putter along the fringe. If the grass mats down you're rubbing with the grain; if it brushes up you're rubbing against the grain.

slides easily and mats down the grass, you're dragging with the grain. If, in dragging, you feel resistance from the grass and the fringe fluffs up the way your own hair would if you were to brush it the wrong way, then you're dragging against the grain. (Incidentally, be sure you do this dragging on the fringe and not on the green. On the green it's against Rule 35-1F.)

A quick inspection of the putting cup will verify your findings. On the up-grain side of the hole tiny blades of grass will extend over the cup. On the down-grain side the edge may be worn, from balls hitting into it.

Other grain thoughts to keep in mind: Grain usually leans toward water, especially toward the ocean, and in the East grain is apt to lean toward mountains, too.

Playing the grain is easy. Basically, putts hit with the grain tend to roll faster and require less force than putts hit against the grain, which slow down quickly and demand a solid stroke. An otherwise straight putt will break in the direction the grain grows. Sloping putts, if they break with the grain, will break more than the slope indicates. Conversely, if the grain leans left-to-right and your putting path slopes right-to-left, the grain will lessen the slope's force, and you should play less break.

Strains of Grass

All greens have grains, and all grains affect putts, but some grains are more influential than others. It all depends upon the strain, or species, of grass.

There are two major species of putting grass in America today—bent and Bermuda. Bent derives its name from the fact that it is long-bladed and bends back over itself. On the putting green this means that the ball rolls along the arched blades. Most courses in the North and Midwest have bent-grass greens.

Bermuda is a short, stubby species—the crewcut that is stylish among Southern courses. Of the two grasses, Bermuda is by far the more influential on putts.

A ball rolling along the tips of the stiff Bermuda blades, being transferred from minute stalk to stalk, will be susceptible to those stalks to a greater degree than it will be to the smooth blades of bent grass. So when you play an unfamiliar course, especially one that's well away from home, make it a point to determine the type of grass you're putting on, and adjust accordingly. Always be ready to allow more for the effect of Bermuda grass than you do for bent.

Moisture

As you might expect, the speed and break of a putt is influenced by the moisture of the green. In general, the wetter the grass, the less break you play. Wet greens force you to hit the putt harder than normal, and a hard-hit ball is less susceptible to the contours of the putting surface.

You could almost go by the maxim "The wetter the green, the straighter the putt," were it not for one small wrinkle: Greens with a light cover of dew often putt faster than dry greens. The ball tends to scoot, to ride along quickly on this coat of moisture, and in such cases you should allow for extra break, since you won't have to hit the ball as hard as you normally would.

Wind

In extreme cases, wind can have an effect on your putts. Putting into a 25 m.p.h. headwind calls for a firm stroke and a straighter putt, while a stiff tailwind will call for a softer shot and, sometimes, more borrow—though you should be aware that a tailwind will tend to get the ball moving pretty fast and will blow it straight, thus offsetting the need to play more break. Test the wind before putting, and if it's really strong and blowing directly at the hole, then hit the putt easier *and* play less break, but be aware that this is probably the only time you'll ever combine those two tactics.

Texture

Your putt will also be acted upon by the hardness or softness of the green. When the greens are hard, they're fast, and you should hit the ball easier and play for more break. When they're soft, they're slow, and you should hit your putts harder and with less break.

Hills

Downhill putts, which should be hit gingerly, call for a smooth, easy roll and more allowance for break than do uphill putts, which require a forceful stroke and a faster-starting ball, played with very little borrow.

If you should encounter a long putt with two equal slopes, one to the left and then a last-minute turn right, allow more for the second break. Why? For the same reason you play more break on a downhill putt than an uphill putt: The ball will be moving more slowly when it gets near the hole, and so will be more susceptible to the plane of the green. At the beginning of the putt, the ball will have plenty of velocity, so you don't have to allow for as much break on the first slope.

Time of Day

If you should ever play the same hole twice in one day and have the identical putt once in the early morning and once in the late afternoon, chances are the putts will only *look* the same.

Morning greens tend to be cool and slow (once the aforementioned layer of dew is off). Afternoon greens are dried out, often stamped down by the day's play, and fast. So hit that afternoon putt easier and play a little more break than you did in the morning.

On Housekeeping

In putting, as little as possible should be left to chance. What this means, among other things, is that you should always be sure that your path to the cup is just as clear as you can make it. Do some "housekeeping," as the TV announcers call it. Clear away any leaves, pebbles, bits of sand and debris sitting between your ball and the hole. Repair ball marks (but not spike marks—it's against the Rules), and take note of anything irreparable so that you can make the proper allowances. If there's a big spike mark an inch in front of the hole, give your putt a little extra so that the ball isn't diverted.

Keep your ball clean, and the blade of your putter, too. On the green, cleanliness is next to accuracy.

Herewith, a rundown of the several influences to which putts are susceptible.

Under these circumstances:

Play More Break	Play Less Break
1. Slope	No slope
2. Hard	Soft
3. Dry or Dew-Covered	Wet
4. Grain with slope or in same direction as putt	Grain against slope or direction of putt
5. Crosswind with slope	Crosswind against slope; headwind; strong tailwind
6. Downhill	Uphill
7. Short, bristly (Bermuda) grass	Long, pliable (bent) grass
8. Morning	Afternoon

All of the conditions listed above contribute to the amount of bend and speed a putt must have, but when you come right down to it, the major factor is still the most obvious one: slope. A knowledge of the other elements—grain, texture, moisture, etc.—will help you to fine-tune your green-reading, but if you can't see the slope you'll rarely make the putt.

Slope Reading

Most breaking putts *look* like breaking putts, and these obviously slanted paths to the hole require very little in terms of slope reading. You just guess at the appropriate amount of borrow and then give the ball a pop. Gradually, with experience, you'll come to judge the slope's effect accurately.

The tricky putts are the ones that look level but are not. If you're unsure about a putt—if you suspect it breaks but have no visible proof—double-check yourself in a couple of ways.

First, take a look at the terrain surrounding the green. If the land seems to lean acutely to one side, chances are your putt will dip down in the same direction. This is especially true if the tilt is toward the sea.

Another checkpoint is the cup. All cups are driven in per-

On hard-to-read putts the plumb-bob technique can be very helpful.

pendicular to the ground (at least they *should* be), not to the plane of the green. As a consequence you can often detect the green's slope by inspecting the collar of mud between the cup and the grass. If this collar is thicker on the right of the cup than on the left, the green is higher on the right side than on the left (at least near the hole it is) and you should probably allow for a little last-minute right-to-left bend into the cup. Watch the deliberate and meticulous Gary Player closely; he rarely hits a putt without first taking a good look at the cup.

The Plumb-Bob Method

If the above checks fail to confirm your suspicions, try just one more method—the plumb-bob. Used by about half of the touring pros, and a far smaller proportion of amateurs, plumb-bobbing is the pinnacle of visual how-to and is the ultimate arbiter of those marginal straight-or-break putts.

The first step in using the plumb-bob technique is to determine your dominant eye. The dominant eye is the one with which you see one object superimposed upon another in the same way you see it with two eyes.

To find your dominant eye, assume the "artist's position." Hold your hand straight out, extend your thumb up, and line it up with an object several feet away, a doorknob, for instance, so that your thumb eclipses the object. Now close one eye, and then the other. Switch from your right eye to your left a couple of times. When your thumb seems to jump, you have closed your dominant eye. When it stays on the mark, you are looking through your dominant eye.

Although confusion and misunderstanding surround the plumb-bob method, it's a very easy technique to use. Just stand several feet in back of your ball, as you would to line up a putt. Grasp the putter at the top of the shaft with your thumb and forefinger and let the club suspend like a pendulum.

Now sight things up. Hold the putter so that, when using your dominant eye and looking at the cup, you see the lower end of the putter superimposed on the ball. If, in this situation, the upper half of the putter falls left of the hole, the putt will break *right*; if the shaft falls right of the hole, your putt will break left. If the shaft covers the hole, your suspicions were unfounded: The putt is straight.

"See" the Perfect Putt

In every putt there is a curious transitional stage between lining-up and hitting. The interval of a few seconds in which you're combining the visual and tactile skills is probably the most important step in hitting any putt. It is during this time that your perception takes you one step beyond, into imagination, and you actually visualize the putt going on an ideal path from your putter into the cup.

This vision of the perfect putt should bring together all the green reading you did. It is a final and complete reflection of your best guess on the speed and break of the putt. It is a positive opinion on the putt and should give you inspiration for what is to follow. If you aren't sure, if the vision isn't there, concentrate, think about the distance and slope until you arrive at a putt picture which does give you confidence. When Jack Nicklaus leans motionless over a putt for several seconds, he is going through the visualization trance.

Then just complete the transition from the visual to the tactile side of putting. Take a couple of useful practice swings, making an effort to practice-stroke the same way you want to hit the actual putt. Then go ahead and give it your best stroke. Try to make the vision come to life.

Practice

You can make a lot of mistakes in a round of golf, but if you hold yourself to 30 putts your score probably won't suffer. So practice your putting first, last, and most often. It's half the game of golf and deserves half your time. Here are a couple of thoughts on practice.

To improve your distance judgment and accuracy, try lining

up a putt, hitting it, but not looking up to see where it ended up. Instead, guess at whether you gave it too little, too much, or just the right power. Then check yourself. Work at this until your guesses are always correct and you're always guessing "just right." There's no better way to build touch.

To improve your accuracy, forget everything you've ever heard about that mythical three-foot circle on long putts. Remember, you should try to *sink* putts, not get them close. A good way to sharpen your aim is to go for an object that is smaller than the cup, not larger. Place a coin on the practice green and hit at it—first short putts, then longer ones. If you can hit a coin 25 percent of the time from 10 feet, you can hit the cup on one out of two.

Finally, to build that confident attitude that will trigger aptitude, gear your pre-play practice toward making lots of putts, even if they're only three-footers. It's much better to sink a half-dozen shorties in a row than to make one or two long putts out of several tries. If you can leave the practice green and walk to the first tee with memories of lots of putts rolling into the cup, this buoyant awareness will extend to the first green and you may well sink your first putt. Of course, if you don't sink it, if, indeed, you three-putt, don't lose faith. Stay confident, and they'll start to drop.

Spend plenty of time working on your stroke, your green reading, and, most of all, your attitude. The more putts you hit on the practice green, the fewer you'll hit on the real ones.

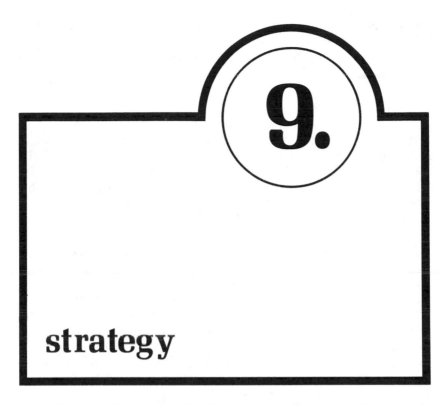

strategy

Scrambling and strategy. At first they don't seem to have much in common. Indeed, scrambling, connoting hurried, harried, almost instinctive movement, seems to be the direct opposite of strategy, a neat, calm, preconceived plan of action. In golf, the second-class image of scrambling has resulted in a distinction which is held almost universally: Strategy is Jack Nicklaus walking a straight line of fairways and greens. Scrambling is One-Putt Harry clambering through a zigzag of tall grass and traps.

And yet to separate scrambling from strategy is both ridiculous and impossible. For the true scrambler is unique among golfers. Every time he steps to the first tee he is ready to do two things: Play his best golf and cope with his worst golf. It is this dual preparedness which marks him as a superbly strategic player.

Every successful general knows that the best laid plans of mice and men do often go awry, and that when they do, he must be equipped with various contingency plans. He must know how to conduct each of these maneuvers, and he must know when each maneuver is most appropriate. The scrambler is no different.

153

He realizes that every round will have its problems, and that when those problems arise, he must have the trouble shots and stroke-savers in his bag. He knows both how and when to hit these shots.

Managing Your Game

Before you can handle a golf course you have to get a grip on your game. This doesn't mean you have to play to a one-digit handicap. You simply have to know your strengths and weaknesses as described in Chapter 1 so that you can match them to the strengths and weaknesses of the course. In so doing, you'll be able to call your own shots, to tell yourself when to be aggressive and when not.

For instance, if you're a big hitter but you have "power to all fields," you should know enough to leave your driver in the bag on the tight holes. Not even the pros hit 14 drivers every round; on some courses, such as Winged Foot and Harbour Town, it's closer to four. All the other teeshots are hit cautiously with fairway woods and irons. So if you're a spray hitter, do your best to get the ball in the fairway, even if you have to come down a couple of clubs. It's better to be 200 yards down the fairway than 240 in the rough. Not only is the lie easier to handle, but the psychological lift—getting a good start on the hole—usually pays dividends on your next shot.

If you hit inaccurate iron shots, but, as is often true with such players, your wedgework and putting are good, you should engage regularly in what we'll call "intentional scrambling." You should play your second shot deliberately short of a par-4 hole that is guarded by traps or water, and then pitch up for your scrambling—and strategic—par. Use a club which, no matter where you hit it, will allow you a safe lie and a pitch to the pin instead of a long explosion or a penalty shot. In order to score well, you have to know not only *how* to hit the ball but *when* and *where* to hit it to best advantage.

These are just examples of the type of game analysis that's possible. A good self-examination includes all facets of the game, from driving and fairway woods to sand play and putting. It also considers the distance, trajectory, and normal shape (right-to-left or left-to-right) of your shots, as well as your mental attitude.

Managing Your Course

If you have a clear, realistic view of your multifaceted ability as a golfer, you can begin your home-course management by mapping out a "personal par" for the 18 holes.

The 15-handicapper is foolish to orient his game around par. He has trouble getting par for two or three holes, so it's ludicrous for him to aim for par on all 18 in one day.

It's better to shoot at a higher figure, a number that is a challenge, but a *realistic* challenge. If your own handicap is 15, shoot for about 83 on a par-72 course. If it's 20, play for an 86.

After establishing your 18-hole goal, break it down and establish personal pars for each of the holes. If you have that 15 handicap, for instance, finagle with your scores until they add up to 83. In allocating strokes, don't pay much attention to the club's rating of the holes. You should be considering your own performance only. If you're a big hitter, you may not want to play for a 6 on the long, wide par 5. However, you may feel comfortable allowing for an extra shot on that short, trap-guarded par 3. If you have a natural draw you may not need a shot on the 420-yard dogleg left, but you may need some slack on the 300-yard dogleg right.

Once you establish these realistic yet challenging target scores for each hole, you can begin to plan your attack on the course. "Attack" is the right word, because if you're gearing your 15 handicap toward an 83 instead of a 72 you shouldn't ever have to "play safe." Playing safe is a destructive principle in that it encourages negative, fearful thinking. By charting your own par you should be able to think and play more aggressively, positively, and confidently. On each tee you'll have the feeling that your target score is within reasonable reach. This confidence alone will take you a long way toward hitting your goal.

As you progress through the round and find that you're even par (personal par) or perhaps even a couple of strokes under instead of 4 or 5 over the actual par, you will be motivated to stay on your game and shoot a good score. Even though you may shoot 48 for nine holes, it's nice to think of it as 1 under your personal par of 49 instead of 12 over par for the course. This positive feeling will help you keep your concentration sharp for the back nine.

Your actual plan of attack should follow a hole-by-hole, shot-by-shot blueprint. The best way to construct this plan is to dissect each hole mentally, by thinking your shots out *backward*, from green to tee. Begin by asking yourself where on the green you'd like your approach shot to land. The exact spot will vary, of course, as pin placements change, but on most greens there's a "fat part," so think in terms of that general area.

Next, decide what part of the fairway will afford you the best and easiest shot to your target on the green. If the fat part (or the pin placement on a particular day) is back left, you will probably want to hit at it from the right side of the fairway so that even a slightly short shot would get to the carpet. If you have a natural draw and the pin is back-left, you will likely want your drive in the left-center of the fairway. This way your second shot can be aimed right so that it will fly over the green during its final descent. If for some reason it doesn't draw, the shot will still catch the green.

The aim spot on the green will thus influence the optimum position for your drive. Of course, other factors should be considered when you're teeing the ball. Sand traps, hazards, and out-of-bounds should be given a wide berth. The best way to do this is to aim away from them. If there is O-B to the right, tee your ball on the right side of the teeing ground and aim for the left-center of the fairway. If the danger lies left, tee the ball left and aim a bit right. The best way to deal with trouble is to avoid it.

Often, in hitting a drive, golfers aim for a general landing spot and disregard what happens to the ball after it hits. This is shortsighted and can lead to unnecessary inconvenience. Drives are subject to the slopes of the terrain just as putts are, and in many cases you should play the break from the tee. Extra thought and planning can make the difference between fairway and rough, par and bogey, winning and losing. It's all part of scrambling—covering all your bets so that you can make the shot that offers the best chance of success.

For every green, every fairway, and every teeing area you should have an optimum position to place your ball. Good golf, it has been said, is like billiards—a game of position in which you're always thinking at least one shot ahead.

This personal plan of attack can help you in several ways. First, as already noted, you'll have an intelligent method for achieving a feasible goal, your personal par. Ultimately, if your plan works well and your game improves, you'll be able to lower your personal goal and adjust your blueprint to something which comes closer to the optimum plan—reaching every green in regulation and then taking two putts. Secondly, and perhaps even more important, by picking apart your course you'll get a clear and concrete idea of its character and requirements.

By considering the optimum teeshot spots as a group you'll be able to tell whether the course favors a right-to-left or left-to-right player—most tracks favor one type or the other. Augusta National, home of the Masters Tournament, is a good example of a course that favors a draw hitter in that several of its holes encourage a right-to-left drive. A prototypical fader's course would be Colonial in Fort Worth, one of America's most back-breaking courses. If you're a chronic slicer playing on a hooker's course, or vice versa, this teeshot list will be graphic proof that you'll never score really well until you change either your swing or your course.

You should also pay close attention to the clubs you need for your tee shots to par 3s and for your optimum fairway shots to the par 4s and 5s. By looking at this list of clubs you can get an idea of the range of shots you have to know how to hit. For example, if you're a long hitter on a short, open course, your list of key clubs may be limited to the driver, the 8- and 9-irons, the wedges, and the putter. A short hitter whose home course is a long one should be pretty good with his fairway-woods and long irons.

You should also be aware of which holes are one-club, two-club, three-club, and even four-club greens. That is, greens which are so deep they can require a range of clubs, depending upon pin placement. The breathtaking ninth hole at the Yale Golf Course in New Haven, Connecticut, has a deep three-level green that can call for as little as a 5-iron or as much as a well-stung 3-wood, according to where the pin is standing. This is a rarity, but three-club greens are not, so know your distances, not only from tee to green, but from the front of the green to the back.

Finally, your game plan should tell you something about that contingency scrambling mentioned at the beginning of this chapter. In mapping your route through the 18 holes you should consider the consequences of all mishit shots, and in so doing focus on the types of trouble you're apt to find. A tree-crowded course means you should know how to maneuver the ball for intentionally high, low, and bending shots. Links-type courses, on the sea, call for an ability to adapt to the British type of play, with low, piercing shots, punched irons, and lots of pitch and runs. If you play a heavily trapped course you'd better know what you're doing when you take the sand wedge in hand. Large greens tell you to practice putting. Small greens demand sharp irons and sharper chip shots.

These course idiosyncrasies are the things the touring pros

concentrate on in their Tuesday and Wednesday practice rounds before the weekly tournaments. You should think about them, too, because you can't plan your overall strategy without planning your scrambling strategy at the same time.

BAD-WEATHER SCRAMBLING

When the weather gets out of hand, every golfer becomes a scrambler, and a decided edge goes to the player who can deal with the elements effectively.

Rain

Into every golfer's life a little rain must fall. Wetness is by far the worst of nature's pranks, and it demands an extra measure of your concentration. Your ability—or lack thereof—as a mudder can make the difference between a pleasant afternoon in the mist and a waterlogged catastrophe.

The first and most important adjustment to make is a mental one: Accept the fact that you're going to lose distance. Slippery grips and wet fairways mean less-than-optimum impact and very little roll. It's futile to try to compensate by slugging at the ball. On the contrary you'll have to swing with less force and greater control. You're going to have to use one club longer than normal, sometimes two, to get the same distance you would on a dry day. Accept this fact of the fairways and you'll have one giant step out of the puddle.

The strategy for playing golf in the rain is the same as for doing almost anything in the rain—keep as dry as possible. An umbrella, while often a cumbersome nuisance, is pretty effective. Perhaps its greatest virtue is in the fact that its spindles provide a great place to hang the single most useful item to the wet-weather golfer—the dry towel. On the really soppy days, take along an extra towel or two to keep your hands and equipment dry. Stow them in your bag until your first towel dampens beyond usefulness.

An extra glove can be a lifesaver. While it may seem extravagant to carry two gloves around, that second one can make a big difference after you've been in the rain for about an hour. If your hands are dry, you'll do fine, even if the rest of you is a sponge. It's also a good idea to carry a handkerchief. Wrapped around the grip of the club, even when damp, it can help greatly in giving you a secure hold. Yes, it's legal.

You should try to dress as comfortably as possible under the circumstances. Rain suits are fine for the diehards, though some of the rubber models can cause you to become as wet from perspiration as you would from the rain. If you have a pullover sweater that's seen better days, it can be very useful. At the end of the round it will weigh about ten times what it did when you teed off, but it will have kept you remarkably dry while allowing plenty of freedom of movement.

A rain hat can serve you in several ways. Obviously, it'll keep your head relatively dry, but it can also keep water from running down your neck and back and planting the seeds of a cold. If you wear glasses, the hat can save your vision. And nothing is more disconcerting than trying to sink a putt as raindrops fall from the end of your nose onto the ball. A hat will improve this situation—at least the drops should miss the ball.

Lastly, do yourself a big favor and buy a pair of rain shoes. They really do keep your feet bone dry, even on the wettest days, and they cost about half what regular leather shoes do. Besides, no one says you have to wear them *only* in the rain. View them as a second pair, which will extend the life of your "varsity" shoes. Whatever shoes you choose, keep them clean while playing in the rain by poking at the spikes with a tee every so often. After the round, let leather shoes dry completely before inserting shoe trees.

Stay under the umbrella as much as possible, and keep your clubs under either a bag cover or a towel. Before playing a shot, follow this regimen: Position the bag under the umbrella and select your club. Re-cover the clubs and dry both the grip and the face of the club you selected. Dry off your hands and then grip the club while you're still under the umbrella. Then, with a minimum of delay, leave the umbrella, address your shot, hit it, and get back under cover.

When hitting a teeshot in the rain, be sure you pick a good solid area in the teeing ground. Take a slightly wider stance than you would on dry ground. This will ensure a strong, well-balanced base and will guard against slipping on the sloppy turf.

Always take one club more than you would under normal conditions, and swing for control, not power. Concentrate especially on your grip. Be sure it's firm at the top of the backswing and throughout impact. Your ultimate objective should be to keep the ball in play, because if there's one thing worse than trouble it's wet trouble.

For shots from the fairway, be they woods or irons, stay with the more-club-but-less-force philosophy. Try to pick the ball more cleanly than you normally would. On wet days moisture fills the grooves of your club and inhibits your ability to put backspin on the ball. The result is a knuckleball similar to the one you get from a flyer lie. So there's no advantage in hitting down on the ball. Often you'll just take a divot the size of a bathmat, and part of it usually hits you in the face. So hit through the ball. Make a long, slow takeaway, and a more flat-footed swing, with little pivot and legwork. Let your hands, arms, and shoulders do most of the swinging. Whenever possible, choose a wood over an iron. The smooth, wide sole of the wooden club makes it less likely to dig into the wet ground.

The fade setup is a good thing to try for iron shots on wet fairways. The open stance enables you to increase loft without hitting down on the ball. Since wet fairways generally make for low-trajectory shots, the extra height can be helpful. A higher shot will also enable you to aim right at the pin and be sure your ball will stop dead. On the low shots it's often hard to guess how the ball will skip and stop on a wet green.

On high iron shots there's usually no trouble stopping the ball. But you're apt to hit a real flyer shot from the wet fairway. So when you get within 150 yards of the green, you may have to take one club *less* than normal to allow for this fast-rising knuckle-ball. In any case, go for the flag, because when it's wet the high shot sits where it hits.

On low chip shots it's a different matter. The ball will skip and skid across the green in much the same way a flat rock skims over water. You can take advantage of this by skipping the ball on purpose—hitting a stiff-wristed, choked-down 4-iron and letting the ball hop and skitter to the hole.

Puddles on the green can present interesting strategy situations for the golfer. First, remember that if you're on the green and there's a puddle between you and the hole, Rule 32-2c entitles you to drop the ball in an area not closer to the hole which affords you a dry route to the cup. If you're *off* the green, you get no help from the rulebook.

In chipping or putting from off the green, one's immediate thought would be to avoid the puddle at all costs. However, if you have a long putt that is dry except for a puddle near the hole, it's not a bad idea to hit for the puddle. Even if you really belt the putt, the ball will stop in the water. Then take relief under the Rules. You'll be left with a gimme after having chipped at a target which was several times the size of the cup.

Putting speed on a wet green can be tough to judge. A light covoring of moisture such as dew will cause the ball to skid along quickly. This means you'll need an easier stroke than usual. However, the opposite effect is usually the case. Your putts will be slower than usual, and you'll have to hit them with more force and less break than dry putts. Don't take a bigger swing, just strike the ball more crisply than usual. One way to get the ball going is to play it more off your left foot. This will force you to hit the ball on your upswing and impart extra overspin. Before hitting any putt in wet weather, be sure both the ball and your putter are free of the mud and crud that clings to everything in the rain.

Finally, the ultimate advice for wet-weather golf: Don't ever play during an electrical storm. Get yourself off the course at the first sign of thunder or lightning.

Wind

Pick up a few blades of grass and toss them into the air. If they fall in any way but straight down, you're playing in a wind. Wind can hinder or help your game, depending on whether you merely contend with it or actually use it.

As with rain, the first adjustment is a mental one. Expect and accept less distance into a headwind, and be ready to aim your shots way off-target—sometimes even out-of-bounds—when you're dealing with crosswinds.

Although different changes are necessary for each type of wind, a few general rules apply to all shots hit on a gusty day.

First, try to establish both the velocity and direction of the wind. Don't go by the old blades-of-grass test alone. Check the nearby trees and bushes, and especially the pin, when it's visible. If you play on a hilly or mountainous course, beware of the ability of the high areas to act as windbreaks. You may feel no wind at all at eye level, but at 8-iron height your ball could be in a gale.

Secondly, be sure your balance is rock-solid. Take a stance that is wider than normal, at least two inches wider than shoulder width.

Thirdly, make your swing smooth and unhurried. Don't try to beat the ball into a headwind or belt it with a tailwind. On the other hand, don't be afraid to swing at it. Just swing naturally, and go for solid contact.

The headwind is the toughest wind to deal with, but the difficulties are more psychological than physical. The idea is to get as much distance as possible without forcing your swing.

Much talk goes on about the optimum teeing height for a shot into the wind. Contrary to popular belief, you should *not* tee the ball low. By doing so you leave yourself open to two errors. One, you may top or miss the ball, especially if you fall victim to the temptation to overswing; and two, the low tee may force you subconsciously to hit down on the ball. Nothing could be worse, for a hard downward blow would impart backspin, causing a high floater that the headwind will beat back in your face.

For the same reasons, you should forget about playing the ball back in your stance and going for one of those low, delayed-rising "wind-cheaters." Sure, those piercing drives look nice, but if you could watch one from the side, you'd notice that after they rise up the wind stops them quickly and they drop almost straight down from their apex, with very little roll. This, again, is due to the backspin you impart when you hit down on a ball that is back in your stance.

Teeing the ball forward is not the answer either. If the ball is up left of your left heel you'll probably catch it on the upswing, and hit a high ball which will go nowhere in a headwind.

Your best bet is to tee the ball normally. Play the ball in the same position you always do, and take a natural but careful swing at it. Concentrate on sweeping squarely into the back of the ball. It will rise higher than the alleged wind-cheater, but if you hit it squarely, the ball will come down on a much more forward angle and you'll get a fair amount of roll.

The one adjustment better players should consider is drawing the ball into a headwind. The draw (see page 77) flies a little lower and rolls farther than a straight ball. However, if you don't hit a natural draw and you aren't confident of hitting one intentionally, go with your own swing.

When hitting fairway woods and irons into the wind, always take at least one more club than normal. But this, in addition to the wider stance and steady swing, should be your only adjustment. By hitting a 3-iron instead of a 4-iron, you'll produce a lower shot that will travel an equal distance. So there's no reason to try to fool mother nature with fancy setups and swing changes. Just be sure you have the right stick, which, incidentally, can be as much as four or five clubs more than you'd use on a still day.

On short iron shots, accuracy of distance becomes very important. Those straight-dropping shots into a headwind can really bury themselves in the sand and rough. For this reason, it's wise to play extremely safe of the hazards. If they guard the front of the green, hit plenty of club. If they lurk in the back, go for the front or middle of the green. If they're on the sides, just try to hit the ball as straight as you can.

Whenever the terrain allows, try to play a run-up shot. For the longer shots (50-150 yards) a punch (page 101) will work for you; from 75 yards in, the pitch-and-run (page 108) can be very effective. Both shots stay low and have less "hang time" than the standard short iron shots.

Never overestimate the power of a tailwind. It is rarely the unmitigated blessing it seems to be.

First of all, a tailwind can actually *reduce* the distance of your shot. Granted, a mild-to-moderate wind at your back will help you, but when it's blowing hard—say 35 m.p.h.—a tailwind has a leveling effect that will force your ball into an early return to earth. On shots to the green a tailwind can be a nuisance, causing lots of overshot greens and big, unwanted bounces.

On the other hand, a tailwind is generally friendlier than its cousin from the opposite direction, and it's much easier to handle. The whole idea is to control yourself. Don't try to kill the ball. You'll get plenty of distance by just swinging smoothly. You may want to position the ball forward in your stance in order to hit a high shot. However, you should resist this temptation if the new address feels at all uncomfortable. Just maintain that wide base and make clean contact. If you're really concerned with getting the ball up, use a 3-wood from the tee. No matter how high or low you hit the ball you'll get extra distance because it'll roll a lot with the wind.

You'll get one more important break when the wind is at your back. The tailwind will minimize your hook or slice. So try to save your worst benders for the downwind holes!

When hitting to the green, figure on using one club less than you normally would. For the short shots, the punch and pitch-and-run are again useful, since they are less apt to blow over the green.

Crosswinds are the true test of the wind player's adaptability. In general there are three good ways to work with a crosswind. The first, simplest, and most obvious of these is to compensate for the wind by aiming the ball in such a way that it blows back toward your objective. Aim right into a right-to-left wind, left into a left-to-right wind.

There's no technique to follow for this method. It's just a matter of practice. But if you can learn to use it effectively, your wind game will be in good shape.

The other two ways involve maneuvering the ball. For extra yardage you might hit a draw with a right-to-left crosswind. The wind would multiply the spin on the ball and would increase bounce and roll, as in a tailwind situation. A fade, when hit with a left-to-right wind, would act similarly. You should be careful on these, however, that there is plenty of room to start and finish the shot. If draw comes to hook, or fade comes to slice, you could blow right off the course.

That's why it's often better to maneuver the ball *against* the crosswind. By drawing into a left-to-right wind or fading into a right-to-left wind, you'll get a shot that holds its line, drifts very little in either direction. However, you have to be honest with yourself before you hit these shots, because they're very tough ones to hit. If you hit a draw or fade naturally, then go ahead. But if you don't, and if you're not a good player, then don't experiment with these shots when the wind is blowing. The mistakes can be extremely costly.

Suppose your draw into the crosswind turns out to be a slice! Such a right-to-right shot into a right-blowing wind will mean a long walk (at best) and probably a reload. So when in doubt, play it kosher. Hit a straight shot, aimed left or right to compensate for the crosswinds. For nine out of ten players that's the only way to fly the ball.

Wind affects short shots just as much as drives. You should be ready to adjust for a gust, even when chipping. Expect a foot or more of sideward blow in a stiff crosswind. To minimize the wind's effect on short shots, play the ball back in your stance and punch the pitches. On chips, hit a mid-iron and let the ball roll onto the green whenever possible.

In stiff winds of any kind, even putting is affected. On long putts, especially, you should allow a little for headwinds, tailwinds, and crosswinds. As usual, it's important to have a stone-steady stance. Arnold Palmer's knock-knees are excellent braces in the wind.

Cold Weather

First of all, keep as warm as possible, without losing too much freedom of movement. As in wet weather, your hands are the most important consideration. Keep them warm by wearing woolen gloves between shots, by carrying hand-warmers, or just by holding them in your pockets or under your arms—but keep them warm.

As for the rest of you, balance warmth and mobility as best you can. Sweaters are generally better than coats because they allow the arms much more freedom. Two sweaters, in fact, are often better than one coat. Of course, golf jackets are also good. Just be certain you have plenty of room. One way to ensure this is to buy the jacket a size larger than you normally take.

For your general health, keep your head covered and your feet warm. For really hard, frozen turf, rubber-treaded shoes or even sneakers can be better than spikes for providing balance.

As on rainy days, you can expect to lose distance in the cold, but there are a couple of things you can do about it. First, take more club. On the bitter-cold days your muscles will stiffen and your extra clothing will impede you, so there's no percentage in swinging hard. Take a long club and a short swing. Also, before you take any swings at a ball, give yourself a warm-up of some kind. Pulled muscles and even broken ribs can befall the polar bear golfer who doesn't give himself time to loosen up.

Another cold-weather trick relates to the kind of golf balls you use and the way you use them. When the temperature drops markedly you're well advised to play a lower-compression ball. If you normally use a 90-compression ball, go to 80; if 100, go to 90 in the winter. The less resilient ball will compress more easily and won't give you that stinging, rocklike feeling that the usual ball would.

Also, keep the ball as warm as possible as you play. Carry it in your pocket or under your arm as you wait to tee off. Rotate two or three balls during a really cold day, taking a warm one from your pocket every couple of holes. Jack Nicklaus does this in hot weather because his golf balls get "mushy" from the plastering he gives them. Interestingly, cold weather causes the same problem—loss of resiliency—and the cure is the same: Just keep rotating balls.

Even if you've made all the proper preparations—you're perfectly clothed, you have a longer club and a shorter ball—you still have to do the hard part, hit the ball.

From the tee just swing easily. Take a three-quarter back-swing for your health as well as accuracy. One good way to get extra distance is to play a draw (see page 77). The low, right-to-left spinning draw will give you plenty of bounce and roll. This shot, as mentioned earlier, is restricted to better players and to players who hit a natural draw.

In cold weather a poorly hit fairway shot can be a painful experience. If you hit a fat shot, you won't get a divot, but something will give—probably your hands and wrists. The club will bounce off the frozen turf and the ball will go just about anywhere. The best way to avoid this is to strive for a sweeping swing rather than a downward hit on the ball. Simply play the ball closer to your left foot. This will force your hands to stay behind the ball at both address and impact and will prevent the shock of a descending hit.

One other thought regarding shots on frozen turf: Be careful in your club selection. The hard ground will give you lots of bounce and roll. So in some cases you won't need that longer club after all.

Hitting middle and short irons from hard fairways to hard greens is, in a word, hard. If the green is fronted by a hazard you'll have to fly the shot onto the green and then hope it stops as soon as possible. When you must do this, try to get the ball as high as possible, since a sharply descending shot will stop faster than one with low trajectory. This assumes, of course, that the greens are not frozen to the texture of concrete. If they are, you might be better off playing short and chipping onto the greens.

To get the high shot, use the fader's address position. Set up to the ball with an open stance. Play the ball a bit forward of where you'd normally have it. Play for more fade than you would on a mild day, because you'll probably hit the ball pretty flush off the hard ground. This will give you lots of left-to-right spin. Expect 5-10 yards of fade on a mid-iron shot.

Of course, if the entrance to the green is open, you can play a low-running shot. The punch (page 101) is best for the outer distances while you should hit a pitch-and-run (page 108) whenever possible around the green.

In cold weather, loss of putting touch is almost inevitable, so you're often reduced to concentrating on the basics: head down, smooth, straight takeaway, solid stroke through the ball. Above all, try to keep your confidence. Remember, everyone is under the same disadvantage. Keep a cool head in cold air and your putting touch may just get hot.

Hot Weather

When the temperature goes up your scores can go down if you handle yourself properly. Don't overeat or overpractice before you play. Dress sensibly in light clothing and a hat. Keep your hands as perspiration-free as possible. Use a towel for this purpose and if you wear a glove, take it off between shots so that it won't become so slippery it's useless. An extra glove for the back nine will give you added confidence the minute you pull it on. If all else fails, get yourself one of the commercial spray adhesives created to make grips tacky. They're available in most pro shops and sporting good stores. For protection against dehydration and sunstroke take a couple of salt tablets before teeing off. Oh yes, hit your ball under trees whenever you can get away with it!

Be aware that in hot weather your muscles will be more loose and elastic, the ball will be warm and resilient, and the fairways will most likely be hard and dry. These facts combined should tell you a couple of things. First, you won't have to swing hard to hit long. Secondly, you probably won't need as much club as on a cool day. This may be the one time when, if you're undecided between two clubs, you should go with the shorter one.

USING THE RULES

There's no reason to scramble if you don't have to. Often the venerable *Rules of Golf* will be able to bail you out of trouble. So it pays to know them well.

You should be especially concerned with Section II of the rulebook, which lists definitions for "ball lost," "casual water," "ground under repair," "hazards," "loose impediments," "obstructions," "out of bounds," "outside agency," and several more important terms. You should also know the Rules and procedures related to these terms, as well as the Rules involving unplayable lies, provisional balls, lifting and dropping, and improving lie and stance.

Do you know all the options open to you if you take an unplayable lie? If not, then learn them. Do you know whether snow is regarded as casual water, as a loose impediment, as both or as neither? If you don't know, it'll do you good to find out.

The Rules contain all kinds of wrinkles which are not only informative but are interesting, even curious. For instance the Rule that deals with a ball lying in the branches of a tree: The

The Rules of Golf will save you more strokes than any other book (with the possible exception of the one you're holding).

Rules allow you to climb the tree and hit it and to jump up and swing at it. Or the one that says if your ball lands in a woodpile you can get a free lift because the wood comes under the definition of material "piled for removal" and, as such, is ground under repair.

Or the one that says if you hit your ball into a trap and it comes to rest next to a banana peel and a candy wrapper you may remove the candy wrapper but not the banana peel. Or the real corker that says if you hit your own bag or caddie with one of your shots you lose the hole, but if you hit your opponent's bag or caddie *he* loses the hole.

You should also know how long the Rules allow you to search for an errant shot and how long you may wait for a lip-hanging putt to drop.

It's your duty to know all of these things, for several reasons. First, so that the course doesn't take unfair advantage of you. Secondly, so you don't cheat yourself. Thirdly, in match play, so your opponent doesn't overstep the Rules without your knowledge. No matter how often or seldom you play golf, you should carry a copy of the *Rules of Golf* in your bag.

In addition to the main body of Rules published yearly by the United States Golf Association, most courses follow a set of their own local rules. For example, on some courses a ball that comes to rest on a dirt road must be played as it lies, while on others local rules permit a drop. When you play a strange course you should always check the back of the scorecard. You may save yourself unnnecessary trouble later in the day.

The Rules are written in a spirit of integrity and fair play. They are intended to protect you, the individual golfer, so you have an obligation to become familiar with them. Copies of the complete Rules, including etiquette, definitions, and appendix covering local rules, are available from the USGA at Golf House, Far Hills, New Jersey, 07931, for fifty cents each.

PRACTICE

Ask yourself how many shots in a round you hit off the fairway and how many you hit from the rough. Chances are at least a third of your tee-to-green shots come from the tall stuff. Now answer this: In an hour of practice, how many balls do you hit out of the rough? Probably none.

The sad truth is that while everyone hits into trouble, no one practices the methods of getting out. It's against human nature—or at least golfing nature—to expect the worst and prepare for it. This is unfortunate because scrambling practice is both helpful and enjoyable.

Every practice session should have a purpose, and there are enough scrambling shots to give you a summer full of one-hour workouts. If you're a better player you should take one day (or several) to learn to hit hooks and draws, experimenting with your stance, grip, and swing until you have good control of the varying degrees of bend. Do the same with fades and slices. When you can hit five shots in a row—a hook, a slice, a draw, a fade, and a straight shot—you know you're playing golf as it was meant to be played.

No matter what your level of ability, you should work on hitting high and low shots and on shortening your grip and backswing to hit half and three-quarter shots. One of the beauties of scrambling is being able to hit about a dozen different shots with the same club—on purpose!

Practice the rough shots, too. Work on creating an upright swing and a descending blow until you realize what it takes for you to get maximum utility with each club. Hit shots from all kinds of lies, in all thicknesses of grass. Lots of swings in the high grass will help you to strengthen your forearms.

Teach yourself to hit out of divots, hardpan, leaves and needles, and shallow water. You'll land in all of them sooner or later, so you might as well know what to do when the time comes. As few as two or three practice shots from water will give you a feel for the shot. In addition you'll gain immeasurable confidence for that once-a-year shot, a shot that can make or break your round.

Apply yourself to the hilly lies, too. Even if you play most of your golf in Florida you'll get an uneven lie now and then. You're kidding yourself if you think you can handle it without some practice.

Try the trick shots once in a while. If you can pull off one of these babies it will have an uplifting effect on you while simultaneously deflating your opponent. Besides, practicing the weird imaginative shots helps keep them in your mind for reference when the appropriate situation arises.

Of course, it goes almost without saying that you should concentrate your practice around the green, and when you do, don't be easy on yourself. Don't hit all level 30-foot chips. Practice from hillsides, clover, rough, and bare lies. Hit pitches, punches, cuts, run-ups, and bank shots. They all work well if you know how to play them.

There's probably no area of the game that benefits more from practice than sand play. You should certainly learn both the explosion and the splash shot, but you should also know how and when to chip and putt from traps. Give yourself not just bad lies but horrible lies. Stamp the ball down, bury it, plug it under the lip, drop it in footprints and under lips, on downhill, uphill, and sidehill lies, and combinations of all these. Give yourself a grueling workout, and you'll walk out of the trap a better, more confident sand player.

Putting is half the game, and you should probably spend half your practice time on it. Practice is the only way you'll develop the touch and confidence so vital to success in "the other game."

The story about Gary Player is told often, but it makes a fitting conclusion to a golf instruction book, especially this one.

Player was competing in the final round of a major tournament when his approach shot landed in a greenside bunker, leaving him on a downhill lie with a shot to a green that sloped away fiercely. To compound his situation, the ball was half-buried and the pin was cut just 10 feet from the opposite lip of the trap. All in all, a virtually impossible situation.

However, if one man in the world could pull off this shot it's Gary Player, and of course he did. The ball exploded to the top of the trap's lip, then trickled the tortuous ten feet and dropped softly into the cup.

A roar rose up from the incredulous gallery, and Player smiled the knowing smile that is masked with a modest shrug.

As Player stepped out of the bunker, one of the nearby spectators shouted, "Boy, you sure were lucky on that one." Player froze for a second, then turned politely to the man and said, "That's right, I was lucky. And the more I practice, the luckier I get!"

INDEX

par-4 comes to res
rds from an ung
ge tree in full bloom
n front of you and in
een—

pens now?

struck 9-iron shot
e and buries itse
arse, steeply b

out?
wing, a s
3-wood